From Ghetto to Community:
The Resurrection of
Afrikan American Institutions

by Billy F. Vance

Front Cover Illustration by Tony Quaid

First Edition

First Printing

CONTENTS

Introduction

INTRODUCTION

From Ghetto to Community examines cultural phenomena. Cultures exist and operate on two levels: on the level of the *individual* **and** on the level of the *collective*, or aggregate. In America, the interests of the individual appear to reign supreme; therefore, culture in this country almost entirely focuses on the individual. Indeed, Afrikan (from an Afrikan frame of reference we use the letter k) Americans have been conditioned to believe in the primacy of the individual; our thoughts and our actions are all too often based on the individualist impulse alone. At the same time, Afrikan Americans have been conditioned to reject, or hold in abeyance, the notion of collectivism. We are blind to the mechanism(s) of collective human action—also known as institutions.

From Ghetto to Community presumes to answer the question, "What are institutions?" A context is necessary to approach this question. *From Ghetto to Community* poses the question, proposes a context, and provides an answer. *From Ghetto to Community* is both *descriptive* and *prescriptive*. The question, "What are institutions?," transcends the individualist impulse. It addresses how Afrikan Americans can assess the current situation of the collective and move forward as a group. Institutions, their role and function in society, alert us to the collective imperative and place the individualist impulse into an appropriate perspective. The purpose of *From Ghetto to Community* is to facilitate right thinking, strategic planning, and collective actions. It explores what should be done now to address the tremendous material disparity that exists between Afrikan Americans and other cultures in America. It outlines a plan of action to deal with our problematic conditions and circumstance.

The Afrikan American collective has two choices. One choice is to establish its own (cultural) objectives and work toward them. The second choice is to default to the objectives of the White dominant culture in America. Clearly, Afrikan American cultural objectives must be at the collective level. Without a collective approach, each Afrikan American individual will default to supporting the cultural objectives of the dominant culture, like it or not.

Embodied in the culture are the social objectives of survival and prosperity. All cultures work toward these objectives in some form or fashion. The dominant culture in America has displayed a distorted interpretation of these objectives: the survival objective is manifested as racism/white supremacy (which is a kind of hate/fear), and the prosperity objective is demonstrated as greed. Since the aim of racism/white supremacy is Black negation, the adoption of these social objectives is out of the question for most Black people. That is where Afrikan Americans stand today. We are people living in a racist society without our own collective objectives or agenda.

(Wo)man has wrestled with the age-old questions, "Why I am I here (on earth)?" or "What is the meaning of life?" These and other basic inquiries have produced great and powerful concepts, philosophies, ideologies, institutions, and civilizations. Today, Afrikan Americans in increasing numbers are wondering, if not asking, "Why I am I here (in America)?" or "What is the meaning or objective of my being here?" These questions must be approached from both individual and collective perspectives. The answers to these questions require an examination and delineation of the context and content of Afrikan American culture through our own eyes.

From Ghetto to Community is for the advocate who believes that Afrikan Americans should be about the *work* of creating a world reality where all members may aspire to and achieve their maximum potential. The intended audiences for this book include people of goodwill of all colors and stripes. It is intended especially for the children of Africa and the African Diaspora whose earthly presence has imbued the world with consciousness, energy, creativity, and a necessary life beat.

Presented within these pages is an approach for framing the critical work of the Afrikan American collective, how to organize to begin this work and how to sustain it over time. It is a basic premise of ***From Ghetto to Community*** that Afrikan Americans have forsaken our sense of the collective. We have forgotten our collective consciousness. Therefore, remembrance of the collective consciousness is a prime objective that will require much work. Such work is not only essential for long term survival and prosperity, but can be rejuvenating in the short term.

Knowledge and consciousness of one's culture (and cultural objectives) are fundamental ingredients to self-definition and self-determination. This is especially true in a representative democracy and a pluralistic society such as America. However, these basic human rights and responsibilities (self-definition and self-determination) have been forcibly and systematically withheld from America's Black population. Why are we here at this place and time? The reasons are as profound and significant as the act of creation itself. We have a duty to understand our existence and purpose for living. These are two attributes that are apparently lost to the collective, now called Afrikan Americans.

What is the foundation upon which values, traditions, and cultures are built? How are they established, refined, and furthered in America? For too long Americans of Afrikan descent have been forced or manipulated into viewing these fundamental issues from the perspective of the dominant culture. Indeed, the only constant of life in America for the Black (wo)man has been the overwhelming, ever present, dank cloak of interference from this dominant culture. Afrikan Americans have witnessed, and even actively participated in, the systematic loss of their birthright through outright thievery, robbery, and/or forfeiture. We must now reclaim our birthright; that birthright, in simple terms, is the ***absolute dominion over our own consciousness.***

There must be a period of cultural development outside the influence and interference of the dominant culture. Now is the time to segregate our minds from negative forces and influences. We must set aside time for some independent thought and inquiry as we move deliberately and enthusiastically to fashion (or synthesize) a society that will work toward the uplift of the so-called "wretched of the earth." Such an undertaking requires a degree of psychological freedom for the individual coupled with a recognition of the role of the collective within American society. We must answer the critical question of the day, ***"Just what are our objectives?"***

Racism/white supremacy permeates, discolors, and pollutes our cultural environment in America and elsewhere. Individuals and groups who are oblivious to racism/white supremacy won't survive or prosper. Awareness of the presence and problem of racism demands that we rid the environment of this toxicity. Such an undertaking requires more than individual effort; it requires *collective* human action. Individual and collective human action is orchestrated through *institutions*. Institutions are the mechanisms for collective human action; it is through institutions that the objectives will be implemented.

A critical examination of Black culture must include a review of the extraordinary historical events that have contributed to the unique present day circumstances. These events include cultural genocide, racial oppression, the breeding of human beings for profit, and all manner of social, economic, and cultural interference by the dominant culture and others. This sorry history was put into motion through the barbarous practice of slavery, perpetrated on people of color by people without color. Central to this grim history is the criminal complicity of the State in its blatant denial of basic human rights to Afrikan Americans. The complicity of the State in the atrocity of slavery, the crime of the millennium, is the basis for Afrikan American demands for reparations.

Unfortunately, this most heinous of crimes remains unresolved, even at this late date. While the U.S. government has dealt with other atrocities, more or less, it has not addressed the crime of slavery. The perpetrators continue to deny responsibility for inflicting cultural damage upon a people. They also have the audacity to condemn and criticize the social circumstances of Afrikan Americans—even though they caused it! The wounds of slavery are so deep and the denial is so pathologically entrenched that, to this day, the government cannot muster the minimal act of a formal apology for the crime of slavery and its aftermath. The State complicity in slavery requires that all Americans, regardless of race, creed or color be willing to right this terrible wrong. All Americans are equally responsible, and must look within, recognize and confront this country's slave past, and the contemporary effects of this past. Afrikan Americans must do this and more.

At this late date, parity is the issue. The aftermath of slavery is racism/white supremacy. Slavery created a unique pattern of history, cultural development, and behavior for most of America's Black citizens. This pattern has resulted in an unacceptable disparity of *life chances* and *life choices* for Afrikan Americans as compared to those of the dominant culture. The disparity is obvious; it is apparent for all to see.

This same disparity, however, can provide Afrikan Americans with a context for collective human action. Disparity tells us clearly what we must do. There have been volumes devoted to describing the problems of Black America, but few provide solutions.

From Ghetto to Community puts the problems of Black America into a context of culture and objectives. It provides a framework for focused thought, constructive dialogue, meaningful reflection, and concerted action. *From Ghetto to Community* bridges the gulf of disparity with knowledge of the individual and collective selves and the environment in which we find ourselves. In essence, what is needed to achieve parity is an *institutional response*.

This volume attempts to:

(1) address issues related to the *life chances* and *life choices* of Afrikan Americans, and

(2) inform and seek consensus on selected *terms of references* that are related to our survival and/or prosperity. The book's essential structure rests on four components:

Culture: Strategic or overall objectives
Parity: Tactical or immediate objectives
The American Cultural Environment:
Environmental impact on the individual
Institutions: Build strong communities

In Chapter One, "Culture," we define and explore a culture that we can live with. We will look at American culture through ebony eyes and describe the impact of living in America on the Afrikan American individual and collective. Before Afrikan Americans can begin to think as collective, we must define our group, our culture. The reader is asked to critically examine the definition of culture as presented, for it lays the development of a healthy community.

The purpose of Chapter Two, "Parity and Beyond," is to show objectively where we stand within the social, economic, and cultural milieu of American society. The central proposition within this chapter is that the life chances and life choices of Afrikan Americans are limited by a great disparity which exists within society. We examine the genesis of this disparity, and we discuss the failure of American institutions to respond to the needs of Black citizens. We then show how the notion of parity, as a philosophy, a mindset, and an objective, may be used to propel the Afrikan American collective to its rightful place in American society.

Chapter Three, "The American Cultural Environment: Of Paradox and Dichotomy," explores the racial situation in America and highlights the impact of racism/white supremacy on the Afrikan American individual. This section introduces the concept of psychological taxation, a type of tax levied against Black people. Psychological taxation is the cost of living in a racist society. Mainly, this chapter speaks to various dichotomies prevalent in American society which impact the Afrikan American mindset. The chapter attempts to elucidate a modus operandi used by America's dominant culture to control discourse, modulate behavior, and maintain advantaged positions.

The purpose of Chapter Four, "Institutions Build Strong Communities," is to pull together the previous chapters into a unified approach to living and problem solving at the collective level. The term institution is defined, and the notion of an institutional infrastructure is reintroduced. To move from **ghetto to community** will require building institutions grounded in Afrikan America culture.

Additional subjects are discussed and placed into a context for Afrikan American consideration, including the role of a knowledge system, knowledge production, and the relationship of information and technology to culture. The case is made that there is a void of institutions and therefore a void of collective human action on our part. This void is the central issue facing Afrikan Americans today. Finally, essential attributes for Afrikan American institutions are presented, and methods for the establishment or resurrection of an Afrikan American institutional infrastructure are suggested.

As we perfect a world view, Black people must have a common frame of reference. That frame of reference must be one that is not imposed from outside our group, but created within it. We must continually assess the sources of the principles and concepts that guide our lives. We examine the definitions of many words and ferret out those meanings that are relevant to Afrikan Americans. We must be precise in our use of the English language and understand that the dominant culture in America uses this language on operational and symbolic levels to convey messages and concepts which support their agenda, often to our detriment. Ambiguity, in support of duplicity, is built into this language; so we must be careful. Americans of Afrikan descent should take care to ensure that certain words and concepts that we use are clearly and completely understood by others in our cultural group. We must also critically review what is said by the dominant culture. These are essential survival skills. Within *From Ghetto to Community*, we seek to establish terms of reference that we can agree on as they relate to the uplift, enlightenment, and the day-to-day functions within our community.

Terms of reference, when properly applied, can lend substance to our past, meaning to our present, and serve as guidepost through an uncharted future. Indeed, terms of reference are a necessary precondition to unity and progress. Without them, we are vulnerable to wholesale manipulation by the instruments of the dominant society (i.e., the media, the government, and others) which seek to thwart the Black (wo)man's cultural development in a vain attempt to maintain both advantage and control. Terms of reference are the first line of defense against the tyranny of the majority, or the destructive bent and potential of the mob mentality. The tyranny of the majority and the mob mentality are the ultimate threats in a so-called democratic society.

There is a body of knowledge that every American of Afrikan descent must know. This body of knowledge encompasses historical and contemporary issues which impact the life chances and life choices of Afrikan Americans. It includes: wealth, health, education, livelihood (jobs) and enterprise (business), politics, law and justice, security and defense, entertainment, rest and relaxation, and interpersonal relationships. The need is to articulate and define issues, ideas, events, problems, and solutions from the perspective of Afrikan Americans. Applying this body of knowledge toward positive action is an essential step.

Dr. Carter G. Woodson, the Father of Negro History, and the author of *The Mis-education of the Negro,* said that the education system in America is flawed and biased. From the Afrikan American standpoint, it is really a system of miseducation, since all things taught are from the perspective of others, geared to the circumstance of others, and designed to foster and enhance the cause of others—too often at the expense of Afrikan Americans.

By focusing on education, Dr. Woodson introduced us to an elegant and fundamental truth of American life: Black people have arrived at this place in time via a fundamentally different route than any Americans before or since. Our circumstance is not the result of some "immigrant experience"; rather, our circumstance is the result of a horrid slave experience. Because of slavery and its aftermath (the maafa), there is a difference between Afrikan American and the dominant cultural conditions in America.

The term "maafa," as put forth by author Marimba Ani, refers to slavery and its aftermath. This is critical terminology because the dominant culture attempts to put distance between itself and the atrocity of slavery by relegating it to the past. The truth is, America had formal slavery from 1619 until 1865. From that latter date America proceeded to oppress, exploit, and terrorize its Black citizens. This continues to the present day. This history of oppression, exploitation, and terror has caused grievous psychological and cultural damage as well as material disparity to the Afrikan American individual and collective. It is recommended that Afrikan Americans use the term maafa to describe the atrocity of slavery and its continuing effects.

The differences in material circumstances are so profound and significant that they warrant extraordinary measures to achieve equality and justice. These extraordinary measures, according to the Woodsonian model, must start with the system of education. To be more precise, uneducated Black folks must be correctly educated, and most educated Black folk must be reeducated. We must be educated and reeducated so that we can begin to define our own reality from the Afrikan American viewpoint. We must also apply our education to the benefit of those in need (i.e., fellow Black people) and to the entire world.

We must be forever mindful that the dimensions of our concern and consideration are at least twofold. On one hand, there is the domestic imperative that we have briefly touched upon; at the same time, the Afrikan American perspective must be expanded to include an examination of the activities of Africa and all children of the Afrikan Diaspora worldwide. These activities must be incorporated into a unified world view. Romanticism aside, we hold a common destiny with Africa and the children of the Afrikan Diaspora; our common condition dictates this. We must help one another heal from the quagmire of global racism.

CHAPTER ONE

Culture

Introduction

The definition of culture is the foundation of this discussion of the Afrikan American condition. Definitions of culture tend to be complex, convoluted, and/or confusing. They are often generalized to such a degree that important considerations regarding a particular group of people might pass through the filter undetected. Afrikan American culture is unique, given the maafa (slavery and its aftermath). Thus, the definition of culture will also be out of the ordinary.

The Meaning and Definition of Culture

What is culture? The mere mention of the word culture evokes images of the arts, theater, music, and dance. However, these things are not culture. They are the outward manifestations of it. These things represent the business aspects of culture. This is where the cultural wares of a people are displayed and made available for ravenous consumption and/or avid exploitation by other people (usually for a tidy sum, I might add!). Yet the aesthetic aspects of culture are undeniably potent and significant to human society. This is so because the outward manifestations of culture, and the institutions they represent, are the principal methods by which things of cultural value are exposed and transmitted to others. This applies both within and outside the group in question. While we could elaborate endlessly on the import and impact of the surface manifestations of culture, let us resist and probe deeper.

A sociologist might define culture as societal organization or the manner by which people are ordered in a given society. The biologist must grow his microorganisms in a "culture." Anthropologists generally view a culture as a collection of people within a civilization. Throughout, however, an essential meaning of culture is one of growth, development, or improvement.

It is perhaps through the eyes of the anthropologist that the most revealing and relevant view of the mosaic that is culture emerges. A notable Afrikan American in this number includes the multi-talented scholar, philosopher, writer, and social critic, Alain Locke. Although not formally trained in the field of anthropology, Locke devoted his life to defining the race and to nation building. His writings on the nature of cultural values and the distinction between race and culture represent profound and timeless philosophical formulations. Locke and other anthropologists, such as Zora Neale Hurston, seem to suggest that culture is "organized self-expression." The notion of culture as behavior is a constant theme in the thoughts and writings of Afrikan Americans. Examples date from David Walker's "Appeals" through DuBois' "Dusk of Dawn" to the contemporary works of Drs. Yosef ben-Jochannan, Asa Hilliard, Na'im Akbar, Marimba Ani, and Molefi Asante. From the works of these brilliant Black folk one can synthesize a practical definition of culture that is universally suited to the circumstances of Afrikan Americans today.

Culture is simply how we get along with one another and how our group gets along with other cultural and ethnic groups in American society. The key here is *behavior!* Accordingly, the following is offered as a lay person's definition of culture:

"Culture is our individual and collective behavior which enables us to survive and prosper."

Such behavior must be tempered by accepted group values and traditions. This simple definition of culture is important and relevant because it seeks to address a persistent, yet subtle, opponent to Afrikan American progress—*the legacy of slavery*. Slavery suppressed self-expression. This violent suppression occurred over centuries, and we continue to witness its devastating effects on the interpersonal relationships of Black people today. Although the effects are soft peddled in this day and time, make no mistake, slavery was out and out *warfare in the extreme*. The effects of this long-term atrocity remain.

In considering the warlike nature of the "clash" of cultures, first, any behavior that does not meet the fundamental standards of the definition is considered *anti-cultural* behavior. Such behavior must be changed, or otherwise expunged, in the interest of ourselves and those generations to follow. Any behavior, intentional or unintentional, which works to negate or undermine the cultural objectives of survival and prosperity must be eliminated. Second, behavior that seeks to supplant African or Afrikan American culture with another culture (i.e., the dominant culture) is considered *counter cultural* behavior. Counter cultural behavior may be viewed as an act of war (if it emanates from without) or treason (if it emanates from within).

To paraphrase an old saying, nature abhors a cultural vacuum, yet that is the legacy of slavery. Where the rules governing behavior (i.e., culture) have been weakened, we can expect abhorrent behaviors to emerge to fill the void. This could explain the plague of crime, violence, drugs, and other maladies affecting our neighborhoods. We must never forget the linkage between our present circumstances and the history of unparalleled oppression and exploitation we have experienced in America.

The descendants of the dominant culture inherited wealth as a result of slavery; Afrikan Americans inherited mistrust (primarily of each other)! The spiritual discord is the root cause of the crippling inability of Afrikan Americans to come together in sufficient numbers and systematically work through our problems (except on a very modest scale or in a crisis). Given the very real threat to our continued survival and prosperity, such mistrust is a twisted luxury we can no longer afford. It is a tragic fact that slavery destroyed trust among us, fractured interpersonal relationships, and distorted behavior. These cultural ills, having been reinforced over the years, are deeply rooted and operate somewhat below the level of consciousness. In spite of the pain, we must bring these negative patterns of behavior to full consciousness and move to correct them.

Culture in the Micro and the Macro: An Analogy to the Economic Model

In the study and praxis of economics, the "micro" view deals with aspects of the individual, and the "macro" view deals with aggregates. The same is true of culture. Micro-culture is concerned with the individual—individual families, communities, or other forms of individual organization. Macro-culture is concerned with the collective, with the aggregate. Our collective existence is as real and significant as our individual existence. As in economics, the rules governing the micro-culture are very different from the rules governing the macro-culture. Macro-cultural rules are established and made manifest through institutions. All too often, this distinction goes unrecognized. An example is the emergence of so-called Black conservatives speaking from a micro-cultural vantage point, making ridiculous assertions about "pulling one's self up by the bootstrap." They often hold themselves up as examples of the ability to "make it, in spite of the odds." What they are doing is making micro-cultural assertions, while attempting to apply them to the aggregate (i.e., to the macro-culture). Even if there is a grain of truth in the assertions, the impact and import of the macro-cultural considerations are usually overlooked or ignored.

No astute businessperson would overlook or ignore the obvious impact of macro-economics on his or her individual business. Nor would (s)he attempt to apply micro rules to a macro situation, or vice versa. To do so would surely mean business failure, bankruptcy, and/or a loss of credibility. It is interesting to note that this is the usual fate of the Black conservative as he seeks legitimacy within the Afrikan American community. By ignoring the macro considerations of culture, the rhetoric of the Black conservative is made instantaneously mute, morally and culturally bankrupt, and without credibility. His or her rhetoric is recognized for what it is: a form of self-hatred.

In the economy, there is a common medium of exchange in both the micro and the macro economic environments— money. The medium of exchange in the cultural realm is goodwill; this is so in both micro-culture and macro-culture. Yet, it is the commodity of goodwill that we find greatly lacking within the dominant culture and, for different reasons, in our own. Paradoxically, Afrikan Americans often extend goodwill to those outside our community more readily than to those within our community. Behavior such as this is indicative of the individual's view of himself relative to other individuals within the culture, and of the culture as a whole (i.e., the collective); it is a form of self-hatred borne of the maafa. Too often this self-hatred is directed at oneself, at other individuals within the culture, and/or at the collective. The notion of self-hatred directed at oneself is often denied.

So, individual Black folk must be mindful that while they may be working at the micro-cultural level with some degree of success, there is another ball game in town called macro-culture. The rules in the macro-cultural game are very different (it is, after all, a different ball game). If there is not a sufficient level of effort afforded to the macro-culture, then the micro-cultural activities and accomplishments may be jeopardized. Indeed, we all have a vested interest in the conduct and fate of the collective.

The Role of Institutions

The argument can be made that from slavery and its subsequent oppression and exploitation has emerged a wholly new people, a new and comparatively immature culture. By what standard immature? The measure of cultural maturity lies not only in the expressed values of the people concerned, but also in the efficiency and effectiveness of its institutions. ***Cultures are sustained and perpetuated through institutions***. It is undeniable that different African ethnicities were brought violently together by the brute force and trauma of slavery. Over the decades, Afrikan Americans have made the strategic error of relying more on the messenger and too little on the message and building institution and community. The problem here is that, unlike institutions, a single personality seldom transcends one generation. If the cultural aspirations of the community are embodied in a person, then his or her demise (i.e., death or some other form of negation) may thwart, retard, even truncate cultural development. Succeeding generations must, therefore, secure for themselves what previous generations had already won. Consequently, a vicious cycle of reinventing the wheel ensues, with the net effect being a slowed rate of cultural development. Garvey, King, Malcolm X, and a countless number of other "lesser" leaders are witnesses to this fact.

The "macro"culture is the providence of institutions. As you take inventory of the social, political, financial, religious, and scientific institutions concerned with or devoted to our survival and prosperity, what do you see? Above all else, a clear and crying need for concerted and deliberate efforts to establish and maintain institutions. As we undertake this task, a premium should be placed on those institutions concerned with the teaching and learning of appropriate behaviors, such as demonstrated in families, schools, the church, etc.

CHAPTER TWO

Parity and Beyond

Introduction

Contemporary striving of Afrikan Americans can be described best as the quest, if not demand, for parity. What is parity? Essentially, parity states that when we consider the things that matter, there should not be any appreciable statistical difference between Afrikan Americans and other cultures within our society. As we consider the things that matter, we must start with the distribution of wealth and include issues of health, education, law, politics and justice, enterprise and livelihood, interpersonal relationships, defense and security, and, entertainment, rest and relaxation. If we are living in a "color-blind" [sic] society as some would contend, then it is encumbered on society to ensure parity and to eradicate disparity by any means necessary.

Parity is a means and not an end. It is ***the process of establishing realizable cultural goals and placing the weight of the community behind their achievement.*** The material manifestation of parity between and among cultures requires collective human action. The demand for parity is not confined to the borders of the United States; Afrikan Americans should move toward parity for all children of the Afrikan Diaspora. In this way, parity will help us contribute to the healing of the world. This world needs healing. A sizable portion of the world's population lives in abject poverty; this population is overwhelmingly non-white. By comparison, the white population possesses a wealth that is vastly out of proportion to their professed needs. It is a wealth that is largely ill-gotten and misused. Something is wrong with this picture.

This is great disparity. There is a striking disparity that exists in America; this disparity negatively impacts the life chances and life choices of a majority of America's Black citizenry. The great disparity sets Afrikan Americans apart from other ethnic and racial groups in American society. The disparity also negatively impacts Afrikan American relationships, including interpersonal relationships. For Americans of Afrikan descent, the disparity unduly complicates the pursuit of life, liberty, and happiness for oneself and one's posterity.

Inequity is a fundamental fact of life owing to chance and circumstance, so mere inequity is not the focus here. The disparity of which we seek to illuminate (and to redress) is made and perpetuated by men, white and Black. The great disparity is an outgrowth of the unprovoked and unjust maafa waged against people of color by people without color, and we are within the maafa still. The great disparity is historical and contemporary; while it has changed in form and praxis over time, its essential characteristics of white superiority and Black subordination persist, to this very day.

The disparity makes a mockery of the notion of equality or a color blind society, or multi-cultural. No rational, sane mind can view the disparity and claim equality or color-blindness. Only sick minds engage in such follies. In America, white people are the haves and Black people are the have-nots. While individual examples to the contrary may be pointed out, this is the true situation to an overwhelming extent and in the aggregate.

What follows is a view of the causes and effects of the great disparity, a view that shows how much the dominant culture is in serious, if not pathological, denial. An admission of the horrible crimes of slavery is an admission of the inhumanity of which the dominant culture is capable of metering out. Denial is also motivated by the desire to maintain an advantageous position in life. When will America recognize and own up to the damage it has wrought upon its Black citizens? This is a precondition to this nation reaching its potential greatness.

In the Wake of the Atrocity

What was, and is, the nature of America's own holocaust? In a word, *atrocious!* America established and maintained the wretched institution of slavery for 244 years. At the inception of the African slave trade, the white world was considered civilized, yet this peculiar institution emerged. And what was this institution about? State-sponsored kidnaping, terrorism, genocide, rapes, murders, forced labor, denial of fundamental human rights and dignity, and attempted cultural annihilation. It was war against an unarmed enemy.

Cultural annihilation resulted in Black people being forcibly, violently, and continually denied the essential tools for survival and prosperity in an alien environment. This included the denial of native language, custom and traditions, of basic education, reading and writing skills, and security and safety. Black people were intentionally destabilized as a means of control and denied the fruits of their labors (e.g., rights) for hundreds of years! These are some of the state-sponsored crimes which led to the great disparity, crimes visited upon the children of Africa by the so-called dominant culture.

Is it any wonder that Black people were unable to secure their birthright in America at the so-called end of slavery? All the atrocities mentioned above continued *after* the end of slavery. In other words, the patterns of behavior in both Black and White people that were established and reinforced over hundreds of years did not disappear over night with so-called emancipation; in fact, they are with us still and will be with us until a deliberate and sustained effort is made to set things right.

As we view the past from the vantage point of the present, the disparities between Afrikan Americans and the dominant culture are significant. Some try to blame Black people; but the cause can be linked to State-sponsored atrocities before, during and after slavery. The issue is not who is at fault for the condition of Black America; rather the issue is understanding the truth about our journey.

And We Too Shall Never Forget

It is popular for those in the dominant culture to dis-avow any responsibility for slavery and its aftermath. The familiar refrain is "I (as an individual) have never dis-criminated against anyone, and therefore should not be part of any remedy designed to mitigate the negative effects of discrimination." Indeed, some Black folks, wishing very much to push the slavery experience from the mind, sup-port these views.

What these folk, Black and White, fail to understand is that the Black case is against the *State* for its complicity in the atrocities of slavery. To the extent that individuals, Black and White, are a part of the State, they are respon-sible. The Black citizen today is as responsible for sla-very and its aftermath as the White, Red, Yellow, or Brown citizen of today. Due to State complicity, we are all re-sponsible and should be willing to meet the obligation.

Black people were enslaved as a group and discrimi-nated against on a wholesale basis after the end of slavery through to the present. Whites as a group, and as a State, benefited on a wholesale basis from slave labor and from the inability of Black people to hold, own, and accumulate property by law. Whites benefited from the systematic and State-sponsored elimination of Black competition. Competition from Black people was effectively eliminated through the denial of the right to own businesses, to come and go securely, to get an education, and to live without an overbearing, oppressive system constraining every aspect of human existence. Yes, Black people have been (and are) systematically prohibited by individual and State-sponsored actions from fair competition with Whites. Thus, a great material disparity exists between the two cultures.

The State has conferred an advantage upon its White citizens at the expense of its Black citizens. It is understandable (not really) that the dominant culture would not own up to the gross atrocity, known as slavery; to do so would threaten its advantaged position. But it is sick that this same dominant culture, led by a conservative, right-wing political apparatus, would attempt to blame the victim for the travesty that they (the members of the dominant culture) have spawned.

Our ancestors cry out for justice. They demand, through us, that this greatest of wrongs be righted and that the perpetrator not get off scot-free. It is in a soulful dialogue reaching back across the pain and suffering and the waste of human potential, that we answer, "And we too shall never forget."

Picturing Parity
Instead of disparity, let us picture parity of life chances and life choices for all of humankind, for parity is our birthright. Parity is our guidepost amid a barrage of

13

misinformation, both intentional and unintentional. Parity supersedes the notion of "having what Whites have." It is the act of naming and claiming what is rightfully ours. Parity involves stepping up to the challenge of building a world that has our signature indelibly inscribed upon her, as did our (fore) fathers and mothers. Parity is about inspiring change through motivation rather than fear (i.e., racism/white supremacy) and greed. It is about the legitimization of compassion and respect. Parity presumes that every culture in the world is worthy, and it seeks to remove the hypocrisy from the statement " . . . that all men are created equal, that they are endowed by their Creator with certain unalienable Rights, that among these are I ife, Liberty and the pursuit of Happiness."

As Afrikan Americans move toward parity, we can anticipate that the dominant culture will seek, at all costs, to maintain its privileged station in society. However, rightness and justice will prevail. Parity will show that scarcity is false and that the wealth is unlimited. Black people need not gain at the expense of White people. When Black children can realize true freedom of opportunity and have available to them a sufficiently broad array of chances and choices in life, the world will see an explosion of creativity and productivity. Parity means that the standard will rise for all.

Parity as Liberty and Liberty as Ideology

The disparity that exists between Afrikan American and the dominant cultures in America can be traced to the maafa. Thus, the unemployment rate for Black males between 18 and 25 years old is 39.8 percent but 6.5 percent for the general population. This 33.6 percent disparity is a direct result of the maafa.

Liberty or freedom, therefore, is the ideological basis for the eradication of disparity. This drive is more necessary today than when similar conditions led to the (un)Civil War between the states. It is what drives us toward parity. It is Liberty or Death!

Vital Signs: Wealth and Other Indices of Disparity

Any discussion of disparity in America must avoid the pitfalls of "stovepipe" analysis. The tendency is to view an instance of disparity in isolation and to ignore or minimize how other aspects may contribute or support that instance. This method of analysis used by Western man fragments, decomposes, and destroys. The alternative is to seek interrelatedness through a holistic approach to any inquiry; this will be our approach.

Wealth is an important factor in Black-White disparity evident today. Parity of wealth would mean that Black people would own a fair share of the means of production. The median wealth for whites in America is $50,000 in contrast to Afrikan Americans with only $5,000. The present day wealth disparity is a direct result of Black oppression and exploitation by the dominant culture. This culture, with the assistance and/or acquiescence of the State, engaged in the centuries-long crime of wealth deprivation. It can be argued that all other indicators of disparity flow from the wealth disparity. As the accompanying chart shows, white net worth is ten times that of Black net worth. In other words, while White people have the freedom to pursue life, liberty, and the pursuit of happiness, Black people have the ability to pursue one tenth of that! The life chances and life choices available to us and our children are reduced before we begin life; this is hardly a level playing field. American society is color blind indeed—blind to fairness and the needs and aspirations of its Black citizens. Almost one third (29.1%) of Black households have a net worth of zero or a negative net worth, while less than one tenth (8.7%) of white households are so situated.

Net worth is one measure of wealth; this is however only a partial measure. There is also the ownership of the means of production to consider. The ownership of the means of production is another aspect of life in American which has been historically denied to Afrikan Americans. As we apply a holistic analysis, we see that the ownership of the means of production not only impacts wealth, it impacts every other index of disparity.

Health refers to the physical, mental, and spiritual well-being of the individual and collective so that Afrikan Americans can live full and productive lives. First we must consider our children and our elders, then those in between. The mortality rate for Black infants in the U.S. is twice that of the dominant culture. The disparity in adult life expectancy is almost a decade; we are sicker, are more likely to go undiagnosed or to be misdiagnosed for an illness or disease. We have less access to health care than our White counterparts. Moreover, there are fewer research initiatives and research dollars directed toward America's Black population. These life and death issues do not even scratch the surface of the health disparity between Afrikan Americans and the dominant culture.

Education refers to the teaching and learning of cultural objectives. The disparity in education deals with *what* is being taught and learned, the options and opportunities for learning, the context and environment(s) for learning, and the ends to which these activities are directed. Much of American education is understandably directed toward the objectives of the dominant culture, objectives previously identified as racism/white supremacy and greed. So from the outset, we would seek to redirect educational activity toward something we can live with, toward our community and its needs. It is not difficult to identify disturbing traditions, patterns, and trends in education. Some contemporary disparities include: the 200 point differential on SAT scores, the three stanine difference on elementary achievement tests, the 20 additional percentage of African American children in special education, and the 25 percent less college graduation rate.

Enterprise (business) is the active participation in the economy through the production and exchange of goods and services. *Livelihood* (jobs) refers to the ability to earn a living and create wealth, while supporting cultural objectives. Perhaps the most serious disparity affecting the ability to build wealth is ownership of the means of production; Black people own few means of production, and therefore, they are cut off from the true fruits of labor. Ownership in manufacturing, service fields, and most other sectors of our economy is either nonexistent or does not approach our percentages in the overall population.

Employment or unemployment rates measure the disparity in livelihood; yet consideration must be given to the quality as well as quantity of jobs. In both cases, there are tremendous disparities between Afrikan Americans and our White counterparts. If having a job confers identity and/or status within society, what then is the fate of the countless number of unemployed men and teenagers. After years, decades, and even generations of joblessness, what is the psychological, emotional, and spiritual state of these unemployed masses? To what extent do these conditions contribute to crime and violence, bitterness and mistrust, extinguished dreams, and truncated lives?

Another measure of wealth disparity is household income. Household liquidity reflects the financial flexibility that is available to a family. Regarding household liquidity, how do Afrikan Americans stack up against their White counterparts? What of economic education? What in the Afrikan American experience prepares us, individually and collectively, for negotiating the challenges of America's economy? Is the economic education curriculum designed to ensure that we are not on the bottom of the totem pole in terms of enterprise and livelihood? Such preparation has not been, nor is it now, a priority for American institutions; they are content with maintaining the consumer culture, or class. Too many Blacks are relegated to the consumer class.

Law refers to the codification of enforceable constraints to be placed on individuals and groups of individuals in support of the cultural objective. *Justice* is the fair, impartial, and equitable application of the law. *Politics* involves interactions among people. Politics also includes the branches of government that create laws and collect and expend public resources. Law, justice, and politics were primary areas of consideration with the civil rights movement, almost to the exclusion of all other areas, particularly economics. The civil right movement failed to secure parity even in the limited areas of law, justice, and politics. They may have achieved their objectives, but those objectives must have been of the most superficial kind. What we now have is a legacy of incomplete work as reflected in:

Disparate sentencing and incarceration rates (indicative of Black people being over-policed and over-prosecuted, while their White counterparts are under-policed and under-prosecuted);

Police forces manned by White psychopaths, whose numbers have been bolstered in recent years with that of Black psychopaths (indicative of the need for psychological screening of police and other law enforcement personnel);

Attempts by Congress and the Supreme Courts to roll back civil rights "gains" can be seen (witness voting rights, affirmative actions, laws attacking public education, etc.).

The disparity within the arenas of politics, law, and justice is best illustrated in the controversy over drug sentencing, particularly possession or sales of powder cocaine versus crack. Both of these substances are cocaine. However, the more affluent (White) users use powder cocaine, while apparently the less affluent (or non White) users use the solid cocaine (crack). The political apparatus (i.e., the Congress of the United States) passed legislation providing for much harsher sentences for those involved with solid cocaine versus powder cocaine. This an obvious example of racism/white supremacy in action. The dominant cultural institutions of law, politics, and justice are replete with examples of this kind of unevenness. It tends to be the rule rather than the exception. Consequently, rooting out disparity in this area will be a challenge, but it is made manageable by achieving parity in all other areas of human activity.

Defense embraces those activities undertaken to assess threats and develop countermeasures to protect and/or preserve the community's way of life. **Security** refers to those implicit and explicit measures directed at the protection of life, quality of life, and property consistent with the law and cultural objectives. We usually associate issues of defense and security with the military establishment. We have largely abrogated responsibility for defense and security to the agents and instrument of the dominant culture; the fox is watching the hen house. Central to an understanding of the disparity in the area of defense and security are the following questions. How safe are we? How safe do we feel? And, are we less safe than Whites? These questions must be asked and answered in the context of the micro- and macro-cultures. We then proceed to define the threats (i.e., safe from what?), and to develop approaches to minimize or negate the threat.

Together, defense and security are the usual responses to war or aggression at any level. It is in this sense that we should focus on defense and security as we consider parity. According to author Neely Fuller, "War, which means any willful and deliberate unjust speech and/or action that is used effectively against any creature."

Is war or aggression being directed against our community or our culture? If so, who's responsible for the war, and who's responsible for the defense? Conversely, are we directing war or aggression against any community or culture? Therein lies the disparity. Racism/white supremacy is, by definition, a war being waged against us by the dominant culture. This war is manifested through individuals and institutions of that culture.

Entertainment, Rest, and Relaxation. This broad area represents activities devoted to the regenerative and recuperative activities of life and living, and the range of choices or options attendant to them. Neely Fuller offers a more expansive definition of his third major area of (people) activity: "Entertainment, which means any activity that is desired and/or "enjoyed," including that which is just and/or unjust, and that which is correct and/or incorrect."

In the context of disparity, the focus is on the chances, choices, and options to partake in the life giving, life enhancing entertainment, rest, and relaxation. This area is not merely about "do Black folk know how to have a good time?" If it were about that we would not be considering the disparity in that arena. The issue is about positive outlets. Outlets where we derive enjoyment and contribute fully to the other essential areas of human activity, for ourselves and our community. It is also about what we teach our children about this arena. For example, the importance of hobbies and how they can contribute not only to enjoyment, but also to discipline and diligence. Given the existing disparity, the options for entertainment, rest, and relaxation are reduced to a pitiful, nonbeneficial few. Afrikan Americans should have positive outlets for entertainment, rest, and relaxation, and these should not be restricted due to disparity.

Interpersonal relationships refer to how we view and respect one another. They are gauged by the degree of trust and effective communication, cooperation, and coordination made manifest in our daily lives. Today, the gauge reflects mistrust, words unspoken, the selfishness of independence, and scattered efforts. The central question is, what is the effect of the maafa on our interpersonal relationships? We judge this by looking at the symptoms. In many respects we have taken on the characteristics of those who oppress us. We allow the devaluation of Black life and achievement, allow expressions of hatred and self-hatred, allow continued oppression and exploitation. These things were a part of slavery; they continue today as intensely as ever. Only the praxis has changed. There is intragroup mistrust borne of a thousand betrayals over hundreds of years. The condition of our interpersonal relationships represents a disparity because it is an insidious impediment with which our White counterparts do not have to contend. This impediment is the result of the maafa perpetrated by the dominant culture. The basis of the fissure in interpersonal relationships is the prototypical conflict between Black man and Black woman, where both were violated by White man, physically, sexually, emotionally, and psychologically. From this nefarious violation, contemplated and carried out innumerable times over the centuries, flow the seed of mistrust. The original poem, *Healing* follows:

Healing
(by Maxine and Billy Vance)

A thousand betrayals. Sold and stolen away.
Betrayed by the Sun? Even as the visible rays
surround, Man and Woman shiver from the cold.
"Where?", she asks; "Where?" he asks.
"Inside!" covered by blankets of ice:
Lies, desires, past, present, whips, chains,
pastel babies, crude neckties, fears,
and faith lost?
"Where?" she asked
"Here" he answered

The ghost of betrayal haunts us as we ask
(man to man, man to woman, and woman to woman)
in an endless circle of blame, "why did you do that?"
and "why did you let that happen?"
We ask these things, yet we know the answer -
"I did it to survive."
After a while, it was not about survival
but about favor, or trinkets, or a myriad of

other things, real or imagined.
And today, I can only say
that I am sorry, and
that I forgive you . . .
. . . and myself.

No other people relate, or fail to relate, to one another like Afrikan Americans. Considering the scope, duration, and perniciousness of the maafa, the fact that we relate to one another at all is remarkable. Our interpersonal relationships represent a special case worthy of the expenditure of our spiritual, intellectual, and fiscal resources to repair the damage of the maafa. Whatever we would build will ultimately flow from and reflect the quality of our interpersonal relationships. As we rebuild and make our relationships "mo` better," we must tread gently, yet deliberately, for we are dealing in a delicate and fragile thing called trust.

The Extension of the Afrikan American Worldview

The quest of Afrikan Americans is not restricted to the geographical or political borders of the United States; our reach is global. Beyond the essential areas of human activity listed above, Afrikan Americans have other areas of interest and spheres of influences—namely, the countries of Africa and the countries to which children of the African Diaspora were dispersed.

It is a general observation that Afrikan Americans, are less knowledgeable of our *continent* of origin than most other Americans are knowledge of their *countries* of origin. This statement speaks volumes as it points out that every other group of Americans can (if they choose) relate to a *country* of origin; most Afrikan Americans are resigned to relate to a *continent* of origin. Even considering the conditions of other children of the African Diaspora, they are typically more aware of us than we are of them. Africa is the Mother Land to us all. We can learn much from, and impart much to, her children, wherever they may be. We need to build into our culture and into our institutions the requirement for a reacquaintance with Africa and her children; this requirement should exist on individual and collective levels. The bridges to Africa did not succumb completely to the ravages of the maafa; we can repair them or build new ones. As we consider the essential areas of human activity here in America, we should extend an overlay to include Africa and her children, in the development of *our* institutions. Key questions include: What is the relationship of Afrikan American disparity to African development? What is the impact of U.S. and foreign national (or international) policies and actions on Africa (i.e., foreign policy, foreign aid). Can we establish a better understanding of ourselves as we consider the history and culture of those ethnicities which slavery brought brutally together to form the (pan) Afrikan America of today?

CHAPTER THREE

The American Cultural Environment

Psychological Taxation: An Introduction

In the previous chapters, discussion centered on the definitions of culture, parity, and how disparity affects the Afrikan American collective. In this chapter we will focus on the impact of America's cultural environment on the individual Afrikan American. As inferred from our definition of culture, things that influence the collective invariably influence the individual. Likewise, things that impact and influence individuals necessarily determine the behavior of the collective. This chapter deals with the micro-cultural issue of *psychological taxation* and its impact on the thoughts and actions of individuals.

At the micro-cultural level, individual Afrikan Americans are subjected to racism by the dominant culture. Racism is not new; it reaches back to the formation of the nation. Thomas Jefferson personifies the depth of America's hypocrisy. He wrote, "All men are created equal . . .," but went to his grave as slave owner. To this day there are those who would attempt to justify such obvious insanity. The paradox of race in America is sadly an enduring characteristic. To the extent that Afrikan Americans accept the paradox of race, we support and promulgate racism/white supremacy; we support our own negation.

The dominant culture seems to gain sustenance from racism and classism. The dichotomies evident in the American culture have conspired to make life in America psychologically problematic for Black citizens. Citizens without color (i.e., members of the dominant culture) are largely exempt from this psychological burden because the dominant culture understands which part of the dichotomy is real and which part is ruse.

What is the explanation for the inadequate collective response from the Afrikan American community to the excesses and dictates of the dominant culture? Dichotomies of the American society serve as potholes on the road of life for Black Americans. Dichotomies cause among other things, an unnecessary degree of psychological stress and distress. This is so because Afrikan Americans wrestle with the dichotomy; we try to understand the meaning of things that so often have no meaning. This activity is not only time consuming and futile, it is also stressful and detrimental to mental, physical, fiscal, and spiritual health. These psychological burdens negatively impact the life chances and life choices of Afrikan Americans. Where dichotomies and contradictions are present, we must learn and then teach how to teach and learn to discern the real and dismiss the ruse.

In this chapter we'll explore a few dichotomies of American life. We will also describe how they "trip us up," mask the truth, and contribute to confusion, inaction, and the psychological taxation of Afrikan Americans. We'll offer remedies, including an institutional response.

Psychological Taxation and Taxation Without Representation

Historically, Americans have understood and reacted to issues regarding money and taxation. The very founding of this nation was predicated on a civil uprising stemming from what the American colonists considered unfair taxation imposed upon them by the British. It is fitting and prophetic that a tax analogy is extended in the present era to describe the effect of racism/white supremacy on Afrikan Americans.

Thus, American society demands a compulsory payment from Black people.

America exacts a price, or tax, from her Black citizenry above and beyond the monetary taxes levied by local, state, and federal governments. This tax is the price of living in a society punctuated by greed and racism, of bigotry and discrimination. Since it taxes the mind, it taxes all other areas of human activity, including health, education, enterprise and livelihood, politics, law and justice, and interpersonal relationships in the following ways:

- When society conspires to emphasize the perceived negatives of Afrikan American people while de-emphasizing the positives. This practice is most notable in the media, but is found in most American institutions.
- When foods in inner city grocery stores are of lower quality and higher price than in White suburbs. Poor food quality taxes mind, body, and purse.
- When our children are not safe in their own neighborhoods, parks or homes.
- When an Afrikan American male enters an elevator and the lady without color reaches for her pocketbook.
- When the nightly news insists on running footage of Black people whenever the subject is negative (crime, welfare, or drugs) although most of those participating in such activities are from the dominant culture.
- When infant mortality of Afrikan Americans is twice that of the dominant culture. Scientists and health care professionals believe that at least a part of this disparity is directly attributed to stress induced through psychological pollution in its various forms.

- When the job or apartment or loan that was available while you were on the phone suddenly becomes unavailable when you appear in person.
- When right-wing institutions spew out propaganda that is blatantly racist and anti-Black. This tactic, as practiced by the Heritage Foundation, American Enterprise Institute, and others, is reminiscent of the Nazi anti-Jewish campaigns of the 1930s and '40s.

Books such as *The Bell Curve* and *Not Out of Africa* continue racist propaganda. In the farce of a book called *The Bell Curve*, the authors attempt to tone down the obvious white supremacist tone of the book by throwing some platitudes to Asians and uses the following faulty logic: that Asians score better than Whites on tests, so we are not racist when we claim that White people are superior to Black people.

Not Out of Africa is a thinly veiled assault on history, common sense, and the Black community. Here the author asserts that Africa has contributed nothing to the development of the modern world. This is a silly assertion when the overwhelming scientific facts show that Africa is not only the origin of humankind, but the cradle of civilization. The author of *Not Out of Africa* would have us believe that the Greeks spontaneously invented knowledge, and that they were not influenced or benefitted from human history and experience to that point!

Silliness aside, books such as these are orchestrated attacks from racist, white supremacist individuals and institutions. The objective is to undermine the impact and achievements of Africans and Afrikan Americans.

As a numerical minority within the body politic of America, lack of representation is ever present for Afrikan

Americans; this concern is political, social, and economic. Historical landmarks in this regard are too many to list, but include:

> *The chattel treatment of human beings as slaves,*
> *The constitutional assertion that a Black person was*
> *3/5 of a man,*
> *The Plessy v. Ferguson Supreme Court decision,*
> *The implications and impetus for the Brown and the*
> *Bakke decisions, etc.*

In a society where the majority rules, a minority (especially a despised, devalued, and/or disrespected one) will catch hell from that majority. Consequently, a Constitution was necessary to protect the interests of the minority in a society where majority rules.

In the current political climate, Afrikan Americans are foregoing the traditional methods of petitioning the State for representation or redress. We are witnessing a wave of conservatism and a tyranny of the affluent (i.e., a complex socioeconomic phenomenon involving the melding of ideological and political interests along class or economic lines). These trends are sweeping the nation and its primary institutions (i.e., the various branches and levels of government, the corporate board rooms, universities, professional schools, etc.). An example of the State capitulating on its responsibility to redress past and present wrongs is the contemporary and historical onslaughts against voting rights by the Republican legislative, judicial, and executive branches of the federal and many state governments.

Psychological taxes are levied, something of value is taken from us, and often we don't even know what is happening. This is the essence of psychological taxation without representation. The lack of representation for the psychologically taxed Afrikan American is a complex and seminal issue. It is complex because it encompasses the full range of human activity in American culture. It is both a micro- and macro-cultural issue. The issue is seminal because it is the seed cause of the material disparity between Afrikan Americans and the dominant culture; this disparity is historical, is related to wealth accumulation (denied to Black people until the recent past), and it extends across all areas of human activity.

In the fight for representation against psychological taxation, individual Black people must go toe to toe against the institutions of the dominant culture. This is no easy task and the outcome is predictably ineffective, at best. Even if the interests of Afrikan Americans were highly defined (they are not) and agreed to by Black people (they are not), we do not have the numbers to influence or change even a fraction of America's institutions. Yet, many feel we must try. Others still believe the dominant culture would somehow change to one that is more magnanimous and inclusive. However, since this has not happened in four hundred plus years, it is strongly advised that Afrikan Americans not hold their individual or collective breaths for this particular scenario to unfold.

At the macro-cultural level, the only reasonable strategy is to fashion an Afrikan American institutional infrastructure of our own to engage, challenge, and negotiate with the institutions of the dominant culture. This must be done while we attempt to impact the existing institutional infrastructure of the dominant culture by leveraging the limited means at our disposal (i.e., elected officials, institutions of influence, and men and women of integrity and conscience within the dominant culture.)

We must recognize that we capitulated on our macro-cultural responsibilities in pursuit of integration. We gave up a modest, yet fully functional institutional infrastructure, built out of necessity in response to segregation and Jim Crowism. We engaged in a folly called integration and, in so doing, we acted as though the institutions of the dominant culture would magically assume responsibility for our hopes and aspirations. We assumed that these institutions would treat us like they treated other Americans. That did not happen and the tragic fact is we have yet to recognize and recover from this most egregious strategic error. Our most important work is development at the macro-cultural level. The need is to develop an African-centered knowledge system and institutional infrastructure. We must address this essential issue for the sake of our posterity, and because our ancestors demand it.

The individual Afrikan American response to psychological taxation varies from apathy, self-condemnation, and self-hatred on the one hand, to appeasement and utter surrender to the dominant culture on the other hand. Still others are seemingly unaffected by the stress and strain of psychological taxation having developed some healthy (or unhealthy) ways to cope. Individual awareness of the environment is the key to psychological tax abatement. Afrikan Americans should be psychologically free to pursue life, liberty, prosperity, and happiness. Awareness can be tantamount to freedom; this is true at the macro- and micro-cultural levels. At the very least, awareness represents a degree of psychological tax relief. Continued unconsciousness results in living life on the edge.

Ultimately, it is what we do, alone or in a group, that counts. Too many individuals who are in a position to contribute to psychological tax relief have chosen to turn their backs on the Black community. This form of selfishness is a luxury we cannot afford. Appeasement and surrender hurt the group. Black people who practice appeasement and surrender are the favorites of the dominant culture (i.e., reminiscent of "house Negroes" during slavery times).

Dichotomies as a Source of Psychological Taxation

Over the years, the schizophrenic nature of Anglo-Saxon society in general and American society in particular, has been chronicled. In word and deed, duplicity seems to be a defining characteristic of the dominant culture, if not a national past time. Our challenge is to recognize the nature of the environment (i.e., hostile, benign, healthy, unhealthy, etc.). Only then can we respond to it and shape it to serve our interests. This is a true meaning of responsibility.

If we accept society's dichotomies, we grant "home field advantage" to the perpetrator; we are "playing on his turf." If we do not accept what is presented we are often left with feelings of confusion, marginality, and guilt. These feelings are particularly acute when we do not buy into popularly held beliefs and stereotypes of the dominant culture. We cannot in good faith, buy into something that is not in our interest, lest we become as schizophrenic and as duplicitous as the dominant culture. Psychological taxation is a by-product of the interaction of the two cultures. It is about the compulsive influences that the dominant culture exerts over the individuals of another culture.

Eight Dichotomies

The challenge is to understand the nature of the eight paradoxes and dichotomies. Note that these eight items represent the short list. American society is replete with all kinds of contradictory and duplicitous thoughts, ideas, and philosophies. These coexist within the same place and simultaneously.

In a recent lecture, Mother/Sister Dr. Marimba Ani, author of the master-work *Yurugu,* muses that when Native Americans uttered the phrase, "White man speaks with a forked tongue," they were referring to his duplicitous nature. So, White duplicity is hardly a new phenomenon. In each dichotomy the dominant culture focuses on one aspect while de-emphasizing and demonizing the other. This process creates the duplicity. It is White self-justification as well as Black negation. We will concern ourselves

Eight Dichotomies Within American Society

1. **Wealth vs. Income:** *The Rise of an Affluent Critical Mass*
2. **Production vs. Consumption:** *An Essential and Required Paradigm Shift*
3. **Individualism vs. Collectivism:** *America's Big, Big Lie*
4. **Race vs. Culture:** *Of the Gene or Of the Meme?*
5. **Conservative vs. Liberal:** *Useless Labels*
6. **Orature vs. Literature:** *Old Habits Die Hard*
7. **Integration vs. Pluralism:** *Are There Distinctions?*
8. **Equality vs. Parity:** *Which One Exists in Nature?*

with the eight dichotomies listed in the accompanying chart. In each example, we clearly state where the emphasis of Afrikan Americans *should* be; we invite the reader to concur. Some of these issues have already been dealt with or will receive further treatment later on in the text.

Dichotomy No. 1.
Wealth vs. Income: The Rise of an Affluent Critical Mass

The "wealth vs. income" issue is perhaps the mother lode of dichotomies within American society. Wealth is undoubtedly the main factor in determining life chances and life choices in America. One would think that an overt emphasis should be placed on wealth. Yet what we see is an emphasis on income; wealth is literally and figuratively being hidden. Let me first explain the difference between income and wealth. Two families have incomes of $50,000. The first family rents and buys a luxury car. The second family buys a house and invests in the stock market. While both families earn the same income, the latter family has more wealth. In addressing wealth and income as a dichotomy and a source of psychological taxation it is crucial to understand the following related points:

(a) the nature of wealth accumulation in capitalist America—one percent of the population owns 48 percent of the wealth;

(b) the relative position of Afrikan Americans as compared to the "dominant" culture in terms of wealth and net worth—Median white wealth is $50,000 while Afrikan American only own $5,000 and one third of Afrikan Americans have no net worth;

(c) why considering income without considering wealth is meaningless;

(d) why and how the notion of income as an index of progress and/or success is a ruse;

(e) why and how "dominant" culture wealth is kept as a hidden secret;

(f) how wealth accumulation over the last quarter of a century altered the body politic and psychic in America to the detriment of Afrikan Americans, and finally

(g) the limitless producibility of wealth.

The median net worth per household for White people is ten times that of Black people. This net worth is not-all inclusive and therefore grossly underestimates the real difference in material wealth between the dominant culture and Americans of Afrikan descent. So, what seems a bad situation is really a worse situation.

Clearly, the disparity in wealth and net worth is a tragic legacy of slavery and slavery's aftermath. Black people were denied the basic right to accumulate, hold on to, and then transfer (through inheritance) the fruit of their labor (wealth). Black people were denied any real participation or involvement in the workings of financial institutions and/or enterprise/industry which manufactures, manages and meters out wealth. Finally, Black people were denied the requisite education to develop for themselves the preconditions for the production and accumulation of wealth. By unjust laws and by custom, the dominant culture trampled the rights of Black people. These immoral acts were State-sponsored, or accomplished with State complicity. Put another way, those in the majority blocked Black participation as the economic structure was established. Herein lies the genesis for the present day disparity in wealth between the "dominant" culture and Afrikan American culture. The sum of these crimes is *deprivation of wealth.*

In a capitalist society, ownership of the means of production is a major factor in the wealth creation/accumulation equation. Black people are sorely underrepresented as owners of the various means of production in the United States. This is due again to the maafa. Should not the degree of ownership of the means of production approximate our numbers in the U.S., i.e., 15 to 20 percent of the total? Should there not be parity in this regard?

The ability to invest has been a potent avenue to wealth accumulation. Investment in privately held corporations, in the stocks of public corporations, and in the endless variety of treasury and municipal bonds are the usual examples. However, one must have something to invest (capital) to travel this road. Also, one must be aware (educated) and have representation in financial institutions to participate in any meaningful and successful way. There is a disparity of financial knowledge that widens the gap between Blacks and Whites. The success of the dominant culture is based on maintaining this informational disparity. It is done through the perpetuation of ignorance. Historically, all of the paths to wealth accumulation have been closed or access tightly regulated against Black people.

The government has been a significant engine of wealth accumulation for the dominant culture while excluding Afrikan Americans. Consider 250 years of government spending going exclusively to Whites. Consider domestic spending, overseas spending, spending for road and building construction, spending for a myriad of other services and goods, and spending for research and development in new and improved technology. The latter is often transferred to private (i.e., White) companies for commercialization. This compounds the amount of wealth created.

The military-industrial complex with its unique form of corporate welfare is a gigantic example of White wealth. Other examples include farm subsidies and the underwriting of just about every industry (i.e., housing, automobiles, semiconductors, telecommunications, etc.) with public funds for private gains. For many, this is the proper role for government. From the Afrikan American perspective, however, it is a continuation of the government complicity to undermine Black economic aspirations and accomplishment (including wealth accumulation).

So, the dominant culture has engaged in a long term con(fidence) game with respect to wealth accumulation; it's a shell game involving wealth and income. White wealth has been amassed, not because of some superior intellect, but their greater numbers and absolute control over the nation's institutions and means of production. The motivations for these actions range from a fear of competition to racism to greed.

Many Afrikan Americans are preoccupied with income and have little appreciation for wealth. Income, not wealth, is used as a measure of progress. There is an income tax, not a wealth tax. For sure there is a disparity between the incomes of Black people and members of the dominant culture. However, while we can readily measure income, wealth is often hidden.

For Afrikan Americans, being a capital-less people in a capitalist society can be psychologically taxing. The situation is too critical for us to be caught in the throes of psychological taxation, worrying about a job, or an income. The focus should be on the creation of institutions and meaningful work and rewarding jobs. The real redeeming quality of the American economy is that the ability to produce wealth is unlimited.

Also, the definition of wealth need not be restricted to the material. The prerequisites for producing wealth are direction, discipline, and diligence in the use and production of knowledge. The application of this knowledge can yield technology that can then become the means of production of the goods and services necessary for our survival and prosperity.

Wealth is real. Income is ruse.

Dichotomy No. 2.
Production vs. Consumption: An Essential and Required Paradigm Shift

In its rhetoric, the dominant cultural rhetoric emphasizes consumption and de-emphasizes production and the ownership of the means of production; the public de-emphasis of production is a ruse. Production of goods and services and the ownership of the means of production is the essence of wealth accumulation in a capitalist society. Afrikan Americans should be participating in economic production and ownership commensurate to our percentage of the general population. Without an appropriate level of production and ownership, Afrikan Americans are guaranteed disproportionate unemployment, substandard living conditions, and the range of maladies associated with poverty.

The denial of full and unencumbered participation in enterprise (business) and livelihood (employment) is historically linked to maafa. All of this is caused by racism/white supremacy. Maafa cannot be relegated to the ash heap of historical trivia. Afrikan Americans today are feeling the reality of how a numerical majority has taken advantage of a numerical minority with tragic results.

Culturally and psychologically, we have been deprived of something more precious than the accumulated wealth necessary for survival and prosperity within this society. Discipline and diligence within Afrikan American culture have suffered as a result of blocked access to the economy. One way to develop individual and social discipline is through full and meaningful participation in the economic workings of the nation. Discipline and diligence are considered by some to be the glue that holds people together. Yet, to the extent that Afrikan Americans have been locked out of the economy, the motivations and rewards of participating have been diminished. Increased ownership of the means of production and increased levels of production are indispensable ingredients to restoring this motivation. The restoration of discipline and diligence within the Afrikan American community is at once an objective and a prerequisite to assuming the mantle of production and acquiring ownership of the means of production.

Consumption is an essential factor of the worldwide economic structure. The world's economic system is, however, one that works toward equilibrium. It seeks balance between production and consumption, capital and labor, etc. Afrikan Americans must fully participate all aspects of the economy. Yet, we are overwhelmingly consumers. This must change.

Consumption in the Black community is exaggerated. This exaggeration may represent a post-traumatic response to America's racist society. Certainly, the maafa was about forcibly exacting free or cheap labor at a time when labor was in short supply and at a premium. It was also about the denial of the one quality that makes us all human, self-expression. After hundreds of years of the Black self being denied, violated, oppressed, and suppressed it is not surprising that the self would seek all manners of outlets of expression. Some of these outlets result in self-expression through the acquisition of things (i.e., materialism and consumerism). Unfortunately, the exaggerated consumption as compared to production or the other factors of the economy is not in balance and therefore works to our disadvantage. If we made or produced the things that we consumed, we could achieve a balance. Balance would mean jobs and livelihood, wealth, discipline and diligence.

The consumption/production dichotomy underscores the need for some basic economic education and a commitment to directed human action. Real experience in economics has been historically denied to a majority of Afrikan Americans. Basic economic concepts such as the nature of capitalism, division of labor, the role and importance of knowledge and information, and the motivation behind human actions and the importance of relationships, all must be taught and learned within our communities. Within the dominant culture, much of this is automatic and a way of life.

Economics is more than just enterprise (business) and livelihood (jobs). Economics reflects of the health and vitality of the interpersonal relationships. Economics is dependent on human relationships and human actions, co-operation and coordination in achieving what is important, desirable, or worthwhile. If interpersonal relationships are dysfunctional, then attempts at economic self-sufficiency will also be lacking. For Afrikan Americans, the maafa distorted and damaged interpersonal relationships; it negatively shaped how we feel about and treat each other.

The production/consumption dichotomy is a source of psychological taxation because a culture that is too consumption-oriented is a pawn, if not a slave, to the market. Shifting from consumption to production will lead to freedom and self-determination. The benefits of true economic participation through production are self-evident. We must be willing to pay the price. As an example, this may require that a premium (i.e., an added cost) be paid for the things Black people produce and sell among ourselves even though the dominant culture's economy produces goods and services at less cost. The difference in costs is the premium we pay.

Shifting from a consumption-oriented culture to a production-oriented culture is no easy task. Essentially, we must learn and then teach one another about the economic system. We must do this with a commitment and dedication of such intensity that it counters the effects of the maafa. We must be fanatical in this regard. The overall effort must be institutionally-based to ensure that the efforts are sustained over time. As with any aspect of the capitalist economy, shifting from a consumption-oriented culture to one that is more production-oriented will be predicated on the quality of interpersonal relationships. The establishment of trust within those relationships is a chief objective.

Production is real. Consumption is ruse.

Dichotomy No. 3.
Individualism vs. Collectivism: America's Big Lie

The dominant culture promotes the notion of the primacy of the individual as professed in these United States. Individualistic myths include "pulling oneself up by his bootstrap," the "American dream," or immigrants arriving on the shores of America with only a hope and a dream and "making it." America speaks of individual rights and liberty, yet a closer examination reveals that America engages in an individual talk and a collective walk.

A hidden hand works to support the members of the dominant culture. This hidden hand moves through the institutional infrastructure of the nation. The infrastructure is a well-honed machine concerned primarily with the production of knowledge, the application of that knowledge (i.e., technology), and influencing and molding behavior—all in support of the survival and prosperity of the dominant culture. This same institutional infrastructure, fueled by racism\white supremacy, works toward the negation of Afrikan Americans.

The dichotomy that arises from emphasizing the individual over the collective is a source of psychological taxation because it is untrue. It goes against the heritage of all people, including Black and the dominant culture. Try as we might, we cannot escape the universal truth: we are our brother's keeper. Afrikan Americans tend to act as lone salmon, attempting to swim upstream against the tide, while the dominant culture edges us on, saying "atta boy." At the same time, the dominant culture is using some high tech salmon escalator to get himself and his kind up the stream. The point is that all the talk about the primacy of the individual is made a reality for the dominant culture *only* because there is a collective mechanism in place and working on their behalf. This mechanism works on behalf of Black folks too, but only to the extent that our conditions and circumstances are the same as those of the dominant culture. Because of the maafa, the conditions and circumstances of Afrikan American culture is vastly different from that of the dominant culture, as measured by disparity.

Preoccupation with individualism has caused us to neglect the instruments of collectivism in America, i.e., institutions. Institutions provide the rules, or the conventions, by which the game of life is played. They are developed in support of a knowledge system that is responsive to the needs and requirements of a people. It is futile to think that the knowledge system of another culture or its institutions will be appropriate for our needs and requirements. God blesses the child who has his own. The institutional infrastructure (i.e., the totality of all institutions

within a society) is the highest form of human collectivism. Until and unless Afrikan Americans embrace the notion of our own knowledge system and associated institutional infrastructure, we will be slaves to disparity; we will also be subjected to psychological taxation without representation.
Collectivism is real. Individualism is ruse.

Dichotomy No. 4.
Race vs. Culture: Of the Gene or Of the Meme?

The defining of the Black race as the "cultural other" is perhaps the single largest contributor to the notion of psychological taxation. It is the interminable dichotomy between the Black and White races which produces racism and therefore psychological taxation. The following is a cursory examination of race and culture; the view is toward reconciling the definitions of the two as they relate to Black folks and psychological taxation.

People survive, evolve, and prosper based on their ability to adapt to their environment. Change is initiated and sustained through the effective use of information. Information is passed from generation to generation through at least two modes: the gene and the meme.

The gene is associated with those immutable human characteristics commonly called race, with the DNA being the primary method of information transfer. The meme is associated with the transfer of information by the mind. The gene is associated with change or adaptation let's say over millenniums; the meme is associated with more rapid change or adaptation, such as would occur within a single generation.

The meme is related to our ability to identify, develop, collect, maintain, disseminate, and use information; it is related to teaching and learning. As more information becomes available to the human species, the meme is overtaking the gene as the more significant mode of crucial information transfer. This point is presented for emphasis only; the actual relationship between gene and meme is much more symbiotic.

In America, we make a big deal of race. The byproduct of a race-centered thought system, racism has levied the psychological taxation endured by too many Black people. Racism is white supremacy in thought, words and deeds. The ever increasing role of the meme over the gene may explain why race is declining in its significance as the determinant factor of life chances and life choices for Black people in America.

It may be argued that, from the Afrikan American perspective, *race has never been the issue.* Our interminable struggle, at the hands of those without color, has been principally a clash of cultures. It has to do more with the meme and less with the gene. The intent here is not to minimize the significance of racism/white supremacy. This disease has been, and is, at the core of much of the world's present day problems. The intent, however, is to draw a distinction between the points of view of Afrikan American culture and the dominant culture.

To view this issue from the dominant cultural perspective, it is very much about the gene. Race/racism is about the gene. According to Dr. Frances Welsing and others, racism/white supremacy flows from the White race's (primordial) *understanding* and *fear* of genetic annihilation. White folk understand on a deep, deep level that a mixing of the races will result in an eradication of their kind. This is a biological fact due to the recessive-ness of the white gene and the dominance of the nonwhite gene. They understand that procreation between Black and White people will create nonwhite and therefore, not "of their kind." This is the paradox that the dominant cul-ture finds itself in; it is a self-made paradox. The concept of race was put in place by the dominant culture. In large measure, American and other European societies are struc-tured around this fact. Black people are slowly coming to the realization that the concept of race is beneficial only to the racist (white supremacist) since it is their invention. Surely this weak concept wasn't devised to assist Black people. Racism/white supremacy is a survival response of the dominant culture. Racist whites act out of their deep psychological conflicts and fears. Racism/white su-premacy is their problem, not ours.

Race has been used as a justification and rationale for abhorrent thoughts, words and deeds by this culture. Black people have been the primary objects of this cleans-ing. The real problem and solution, however, lie within the dominant culture's psyche. It is not something or some-one external to themselves. The ultimate outcome of the cleansing of the dominant culture is unknown, except to say that this culture must love or perish.

Battling the many manifestations of the psychologi-cal malaise known as racism has been, and is, an arduous task. These battles are the result of a war of aggression by the dominant culture against peoples of color. An inevi-table component of this aggression is psychological war-fare and propaganda directed at those classified as the cul-tural other. For Afrikan Americans to react to this psy-chological warfare in a way that reflects their self-doubt, guilt, or shame is inappropriate and injurious to the whole of humanity. In too many instances, we allow racism to dictate our actions and our behavior; we must resist knee-jerk reactions. We must look beyond and behave in ways that are in our best interest.

Culture refers to our individual and collective behavior which enables us to survive and prosper. Behavior is often dependent on quantity and quality of information. The dominant culture in America has greater access to useful information than we do.

This is a form of *information asymmetry*, a key concept in economics and every other area of human activity. Information asymmetry enables those with the informational (or knowledge) advantage to dominate and otherwise rip off those who are at an informational disadvantage. Information asymmetry did not just happen; it was created via the maafa. Members of the dominant culture aggressively prevented Black people from acquiring and using information. In many cases this was accomplished by force. Black people were prevented from using information to develop their culture. Black people were denied the essential tools, mechanisms, and institutions for teaching, learning, surviving, and prospering. This inhuman deprivation is a legacy of the maafa. Racism is a war without a declaration of war, and Americans of Afrikan descent suffer psychological taxation without relief or defense as a result. In the eyes of the dominant culture, the mind is fair game.

This is the case as viewed from the racial perspective. Yet, the concept of race is manmade; it is the tool of the "dominant" culture and has not served the interests of Black people. Race refers to immutable physical human characteristics, while culture refers to human actions (ideally directed toward survival and prosperity). Culture is related to the use of information and to the processes of teaching and learning. Culture is the strength of Afrikan Americans; it is the Creator's divine blessing which only awaits our recognition and acceptance of it.

If less focus was placed on race by Afrikan Americans and more focus placed on culture, then clarity would be possible and psychological warfare, i.e., racism, would be neutralized. We can achieve the following objectives through an Afrikan American functional institutional infrastructure:

(1) engaging and influencing America's institutions on behalf of Afrikan Americans, and
(2) filling the void where the dominant culture's institutions are unwilling or unable to respond to Afrikan American needs.

Culture is real. Race is ruse.

Dichotomy No. 5.
Conservative vs. Liberal: Useless Labels

The preponderance of labels in the American lexicon is enough to give any rational person reason for pause. Nowhere is this more true than in the political realm; politicians and their concubine, the media, have made an art of assigning names, code words, and labels to what should otherwise be substantive ideas, issues, and movements. It is done in the interest of truncating, dumbing down, or adding biases and publicity spins of various forms.

At one time in this nation's history, the terms liberal and conservative meant something (to the dominant culture). Today, however, liberals are discredited and those who profess to be conservatives are merely masquerading. The so-called conservatives have slandered the concept of liberalism through a barrage of misrepresentation, misinformation, and outright lies. These efforts were financed largely through the moneyed interests of the Republican Party, the party of Big Business. In fact, conservatism, as practiced in the United States by the Republican Party, only exists in its opposition to liberalism, the "demon," which the conservatives themselves created. Again, we see the trait of dualism, dichotomy, or more appropriately, schizophrenia.

Liberalism had a glorious past; it stood supreme as an ideology only a generation ago. Liberalism meant inclusiveness, progressivism, and tolerance of others. It was associated with the rights of workers and the disadvantaged in our society. But given the choice of upholding these high and worthy ideals or capitulating to the moneyed interests and the accumulation of wealth, the traditional standardbearers of liberalism capitulated. This resulted in an ideological void filled by conservatives.

Black conservatives apparently feel a kinship with dominant culture conservatives based on the word conservative! Some Black folk think conservatism is the same as tried and true, values, traditions, rituals, and customs. Dominant culture conservatives on the other hand have gotten away from this notion of conservatism. Their focus now seems to be twofold:

(1) the maintenance and increase of accumulated wealth, and
(2) the destruction of liberals and liberalism as an ideology.

We have mentioned that racism/white supremacy and greed are the objectives of the dominant culture. Liberalism has been associated with human and civil rights as well as the redistribution of wealth. These tenets are viewed as a threat to the strategic objectives of the dominant culture. In particular, liberalism is seen as a threat to wealth accumulation; therefore, conservatism is largely a function of greed.

Dominant culture conservatives are more virulent in their views regarding liberals than are the Black people who would call themselves conservatives. There are some Black people who parrot the conservative ideological line of hatred for liberals. They stand out like a neon sign and have zero creditability in the Black community. White conservatives tend to engage in hate-mongering, demagoguery, racial, and ethnic intolerance.

This brand of hatred is often expressed with the euphemism "angry White males." As if White males have something to be angry about! They own more than 90 percent of the wealth of the nation, much of it illegally gained. Dominant culture conservatives are not interested in maintaining or conserving anything but their wealth and advantaged position in this society. They are committed to the negation of liberalism as they themselves have defined it.

If dominant culture conservatives are not practicing conservatism, what then is it engaged in? The behavior of contemporary conservatives is indistinguishable from fascism. In describing fascism, Webster states that it is "a system of government characterized by:

(1) "rigid one-party dictatorship" (the aim of the Republican Party?)

(2) "forcible suppression of the opposition" (witness the attacks on unions, minority groups, etc.)

(3) "the retention of private ownership and production protected under centralized government control" (i.e., the blocking of affirmative action program, the 1996 Telecommunications Act),

(4) "belligerent nationalism and racism, glorification of war." Sounds like the conservatives are well down the road to fascism.

The conservatives are preoccupied with "cutting taxes," reducing the role of government, ending affirmative action programs, ending public assistance, cutting programs for children, undermining the rights of workers, etc. All this by a group of people who already own more than 90 percent of the wealth of the nation and virtually all the means of production; yet, they want more.

This has, over the last fifty years or so, always been the providence and position of the Republican-minded. Recently, it has become the de facto position of the Democratic-minded as well. The dichotomy is complete. Once opposing views and ideologies of a democratic society are now indistinguishable; all is "normal" within the psyche of the dominant culture.

Increasingly, there is a line of demarcation that is drawn along class lines (i.e., rich vs poor), as opposed to political lines (i.e., liberals vs. conservatives or democrats vs. republicans). But the class lines have new labels now with the affluent on one side, the less affluent (or affluent wannabees) on another side, and finally the non-affluent bringing up the rear. The latter group takes the brunt of the attack from the affluent and their agents. Irrespective of labels, the name of the political game today is the affluent

vs the non-affluent. This is how most contemporary political issues break down. Where money is concerned,
there are no conservatives or liberals. Everyone can be
bought with a tax cut here, a little less regulation there, a
book deal down the road, etc. So this is the American way?

In reality, terms such as liberal and conservative are
useless labels with no meaning for Afrikan Americans.
They are words served up as rhetoric by an affluent class
which is growing increasingly isolated and elitist. The
affluent class controls both the wealth of the nation and
the means of production. There is little distinction in the
behavior of affluent conservatives or affluent liberals in
contemporary America. The dichotomy has been perpetuated by the so-called conservative camp to further its own
agenda.

We are confronted by fascism, which represent a clear
and present danger. So, for Afrikan Americans caught up
in this dichotomy of liberal vs. conservative, the advice is
to look beyond your individual self interests as the barom-
eter of the political atmosphere; consider the collective.
Reject the labels that are projected at us; refuse to pick
sides. Look to rightness and fairness, and reap a psychological tax cut.

Principles are real. Labels are ruse.

Dichotomy No. 6.
Orature vs. Literature: Old Habits Die Hard

The dichotomy between orature and literature is not
a benign one; society is very much dependent on both modes
of expression for the successful functioning of all human
activity. Afrikan American culture and the dominant culture

are both wed to an oral tradition that predates any written tradition. However, the dominant culture has expanded its mode of expression to the literary (that is, dependence on the written word). Among other things, this facilitates control and ownership. Afrikan Americans have a strong facility for and attachment to the oral tradition. Our use of the literary mode of expression is in its nascent stage.

The presumption is that today's Afrikan American is the product of many Black people from various ethnic backgrounds from pre-colonial and colonial Africa. It is a further presumption that the societies in Africa from which slaves were taken were primarily oral societies. However, slaves could read and write. The record clearly shows that many who ended up as slaves were very educated and accomplished in the literary mode. Rather, we're looking at the general nature of the societies from which the slaves originated. Given this background, Afrikan Americans may be viewed as being in the midst of a shift from the oral to a written tradition. Such a transition under the best of circumstances would be problematic. For Afrikan Americans the transition has been (and is) under the extreme duress of the maafa, which is arguably, the worst of circumstances. The implications of this transition are enormous, embracing our concepts of intelligence, human discourse, cultural norms, the structure of consciousness, even perhaps, brain physiology.

The dichotomy between oral and written styles of expression is affected by the dominant culture which values a written mode of expression. The notion of permanence associated with the written word is also an important aspect. In the present era, ideas, thoughts, philosophies, or ideologies are codified in the written word. The written word is easier to pass down through time. In *Orality and Literacy*, author Walter J. Ong points out that literacy represents a kind of "autonomous discourse," meaning that in writing, the sender (writer) is made "remote" from the receiver (reader) of the discourse. This remote writer cannot be challenged or questioned directly. Whatever (s)he has written will remain written although the essence of the discourse may have changed or been refuted. In oral discourse, on the other hand, ideas and points of view may be challenged directly and the speaker might support or acquiesce to a challenge. At any rate, some degree of closure is possible between sender and receiver in the oral discourse. Orature is decidedly impermanent, particularly without the benefit of ritual, customs, and tradition to sustain it.

The nature of information and knowledge, coupled with the dispersed nature of society, overwhelms the oral mode of communication. There are many reasons for this, including information technology and the shear volume of information with which one must contend. Yet, the oral mode of expression remains supreme in human discourse and interaction. Orature can stir and move people; while this impact may be ephemeral, it is both potent and important. Orature is an important part of the nature and heritage of Africans and Afrikan Americans. Contemporary lifestyle in America, with its blind eye to ritual and ceremony, diminishes the effectiveness of oral discourse as an instrument of progress. However, orature does have its place. As with most dichotomies, Afrikan Americans must seek an appropriate balance between the oral and the literary. There should be a degree of shifting from the former to the latter if we are to be effective in American society.

Within our community, the oral mode of expression is associated with personalities or individuals (who are "good" speakers or orators). This predates our arrival on the shores of this land. The oral tradition was not lost in the slavery environment. Yet, without the institutions of ritual and ceremony, there is a fleeting nature to the spoken word. This is especially true in an environment of information overload and misinformation. Afrikan Americans should focus away from personalities and toward institutions. Such a refocus would facilitate the necessary balance between orature and literature.

It is given that our objectives are survival and prosperity. Therefore, in the context of our African heritage and Afrikan American present, our future success is hinged on an appropriate balance of both oral and literary modes of self-expression (individually and collectively). The times demand that we recognize and leverage all modes of expression and seek increased efficiency in the application of the human knowledge available to us. Such "productivity" gains, in pursuit of survival and prosperity, require the use of the tools and technology of literacy, in support of both literacy and orature.

There is no reason that technology cannot be effectively leveraged in support of orature. For example, let's align our good speakers with our most important messages (as determined by our knowledge system), digitize them, make them interactive and available to all through the various delivery systems (i.e., inter and intranets, optical storage systems, etc.). Let's seek applications of *our* knowledge system (i.e., technology deemed supportive of Afrikan American cultural objectives) and pass it down to the (wo)man on the street and to our children, in their schools and homes.

Psychological taxation results when there is an improper or inappropriate balance between orature and literature. We do much talking, but what is behind the talk?

We must have structure behind the talk. For our ancestors, structure was provided by tradition, ritual, and ceremony; orature worked well. For us, structure should be provided by institutions, however, we have yet to address this serious issue. Orature is at home in the Black community and should be a source for a psychological tax rebate. Every man, woman, and child of the Black community can relate to the power and passion of the spoken word; literature is embraced by fewer people. Literature is less at home in the Black community, so we must strike that appropriate balance lest we pay a psychological tax.

Orature and Literature are real. The separation of the two is a ruse.

Dichotomy No. 7.
Integration vs. Pluralism: Are There Distinctions?

Integration is a major source of psychological taxation for Afrikan Americans. Integration has been, and is, a ruse. It is a phony and baseless bill of goods sold to Afrikan Americans to achieve someone else's reality. Integration has not worked for Black America. The acceptance of integration by Black people was (is) a strategic mistake whose price was the disintegration of our community and long standing institutions. If such a high price was rendered for integration, then a brief examination of the meaning of the term is not only warranted, but essential. Important questions include: During the integrationist frenzy of the '50s and '60s, did Black people really need integration or was desegregation the objective? Are they the same? What players or stakeholders devised the integration strategy and why? Was integration really the desire of the masses of Black folks? Was integration a realistic objective for Black people in America? If integration has not served our interests, what are some contemporary alternatives?

Integration was the objective and reality of another culture. It came from forces associated with the National Association for the Advancement of Colored People (NAACP). It seems that this organization was largely a front for Jewish aspirations regarding public accommodation, first class citizenship, and professional education, denied them under America's dominant culture. Afrikan Americans aspired these basic human rights as well. Since Jewish Americans did not have sufficient numbers to effectively press its case, an alliance with Black people was a marriage of convenience.

Who really benefited from integration? Integration was an expression of Jewish reality, so much so that Jewish Americans have made the "successful" transition from being "colored people" to being considered White people today. During the period when integration was an issue, Jews were being denied certain human rights, despite their worldwide religious organization, cultural solidarity, and material wealth. Bigotry, religious hatred, and jealousy kept Jews out of the country clubs, certain hotels, ownership of certain properties, and other business deals. Jews were, in a sense, relegated to second class citizenship due to religious and "racial" persecution heaped upon them by the dominant culture. It appears that Jewish Americans wanted to be fully included into mainstream America; Jewish culture, therefore, required a strategy for inclusion or incremental assimilation. That strategy was (is) integration. Black people were a necessary part of this strategy because Jews did not possess the numbers to successfully press their case. Also, they did not have the history or scope of oppression in America to press their case and have the necessary political impact. The vehicle for this strategy was the NAACP.

Certainly, the NAACP has done some excellent work for the Afrikan American community. However, this organization is influenced, unduly so, by forces outside the Black community. Thus, the organization has limited utility for us. It has served the forces of integration well and continues to do so. But, America is not an integrated society, it is a pluralistic society. The Afrikan American community must avoid the type of covert manipulation implicit in the integration debacle. The NAACP is not alone. Unfortunately, organizations, businesses, and individuals that we would otherwise consider to be Black and working in our interests have been coopted to such an extent that they are actually working against us. The clandestine and pernicious nature of this type of subversion and manipulation of the Black collective is particularly disturbing because it represents the selling out of the collective by the individual. This type of activity can be countered or curtailed only if we have men and women of integrity. Within the ranks of our political and business leaders, we have individuals who have been groomed and/or sponsored by forces outside our community. While they may appear to contribute to the Black cause, ultimately they are in place to serve the interests of someone else. This is what happened with integration, and it is even more pervasive and covert today. The notion of integration is a profound source of psychological taxation simply because it is an unrealizable goal in the sense of a group imperative. It represents a dream deferred and the futile expenditure of psychological and social capital for the benefit of others.

Pluralism explains how America works, how it operates. Simply stated, pluralism refers to the interaction and competition between groups, or cultures, within the mosaic known as American society.

Indeed, pluralism does suggest a leveling of the playing field. It represents a condition of harmony and parity between groups. If pluralism is so desirable, why is it not fully embraced by all? There is an inherent incompatibility between pluralism and the global system of white supremacy and domination known as racism.

Those who have achieved positions of status within the society will oppose any ideology or approach that might undermine their advantage, even though the advantaged position or station is ill-gotten. This is the genesis of the present day angry White male. They are angry, or rather fearful, that they may have to compete on equal footing with others (i.e., minorities, women, etc.). In such an environment, what masquerades as merit is only undeserved privilege, thinly disguised. America's dominant culture has so confused merit with privilege that in their eyes, the two are the same.

Racism/white supremacy has produced both a dominant culture in America and a tremendous material disparity between that culture and Afrikan Americans. The notion of a dominant culture obviates the principle of pluralism according to the definition just put forth. Therefore, a balance must be achieved in America and worldwide, so that none of the diverse groups becomes dominant. For Afrikan Americans, this means that we must become competitive through awareness, innovation, organized action, and the tireless pursuit of parity. In this sense, parity is the eradication of the material disparity that exists between Afrikan American culture and other cultures in America.

The pursuit of the unrealizable goal of group integration by the Black (wo)man into racist America is a significant source of psychological taxation; it causes intellectual atrophy and retarded human action. The notion of group integration must be dismissed; it is a misdirected impulse elevated to ideology status. Since there are integration aspirants within the ranks of Black people, let's look at some positive channels or outlets for the integrationist impulse. Integration exists on at least three levels: the individual or personal level, the intra-group level, and as previously stated, the inter-group level.

The previous paragraphs have revealed inter-group integration within American society to be a ruse; this is not a positive outlet for the integrationist impulse. To avoid psychological taxation, integration should never be a group imperative. Individual Afrikan Americans may choose to integrate, but if they do so, it should be undertaken only after achieving integration on the personal level and on an intra-group level.

Pluralism is real. Integration is ruse.

Dichotomy No. 8.
Equality vs. Parity: Which One Exists in Nature?

The term equality is particularly important in the lexicon of race relations. However, the purpose of this dichotomy is to suggest that there may be a problem with the term equality. It is not something we should aspire to. Equality does not exist in nature; it cannot be forced, legislated, or otherwise brought about through human actions. Each snowflake, each leaf, each animal form of life is unique and therefore "unequal." Here, "unequal" does not mean nor does it imply inferior, only different. Nature seems to go out of her way to infuse differences. It is folly to waste time and resources on demands for some ideal form of equality when no one under the sun can deliver on such demand. What we see in nature is a wondrous diversity and balance. As nature's analogy is extended to the social realm of culture, this blend of diversity and balance is captured best in the terms, pluralism and parity.

What we should aspire to is parity. The notion of parity goes hand in hand with the concept of cultural pluralism. Pluralism recognizes the existence of the many cultural or ethnic groups where none is dominant. Parity describes the ideal relationship of the (many) cultures in America's pluralistic society. We have previously stated that parity is the process of establishing realizable cultural goals and placing the weight of the community behind their achievement. The concept of parity suggests that Afrikan Americans should be represented, in all walks of life, proportional to their numbers in the overall population. Parity then becomes the baseline indicator of society's successes or failures to achieve a truly pluralistic culture. Parity is the floor, not the ceiling.

There is no reason for the tremendous material disparity that exists between the dominant culture and Afrikan Americans. Parity, in all positive walks of life, should be our goal, our objective, our philosophy, indeed, our ideology. The call for equal opportunity should be dismissed and replaced with mechanisms to ensure freedom of opportunity and parity. Equality, or the quest for equality, is viewed as an unrealizable goal, and therefore a source of psychological taxation. What can be more taxing than a goal that cannot be achieved? Our striving for equality should be supplanted by a demand and directed action toward parity.
Parity is real. Equality is ruse.

CHAPTER FOUR

Institutions Build Strong Communities

The central problem affecting the Afrikan American collective is the lack of viable institutions and the failure to build communities within the context of America's plural society. Simply put, America is a land of institutions; they are the chief mechanisms of collective human actions. Yet this critical factor is obscured by the incessant notion of individual primacy. The Afrikan American preoccupation with the primacy of the individual, as perpetuated by America's dominant culture, has caused Black people to neglect the importance and necessity of institutions. The dominant culture talks the individual talk, but walks a collective walk.

To address these issues in a meaningful way, it is necessary to delve into the character, nature, culture, and history of American institutions. In this chapter we will:

(1) examine the meaning of the term institution;
(2) re-define institution to suit the needs of Afrikan Americans
(3) explore America's community, which is the totality of institutions.

Afrikan Americans often speak the phrase, "we as a people." This conveys collective thought, words, and actions. Most often, "we as a people" refers to something community members need to do. It refers to behavior or actions directed to some specific end. Yet, what is the mechanism for achieving any collective objective within the context of American life, or within the context of the

Afrikan American community? How are the hopes and aspirations of a group of people translated into sustained human actions? How is human behavior modulated so that a people reap the rewards and fruits of life? How do we minimize or negate those things (thoughts, words, and deeds) which would contribute to our ineffectiveness or our demise? Without exception, these issues are best handled by society's mechanisms for collective human actions—institutions. We are a distinct culture within America's plural society, yet Afrikan Americans have few organizational structures that represent all, or even a majority, of us. What we have instead is an unhealthy reliance on the organizational structures of the dominant culture.

Those within the Afrikan American community who say "we as a people" are on the right track. For the use of this phrase suggests a recognition of at least two things. First is the need for collective action. Second is the apparent lack within the Afrikan American community of a viable mechanism to achieve any real or sustained collective actions. This sets us apart from other cultural and ethnic groups in America. Within the Afrikan American community, there is a void of institutions in terms of quantity, quality, and foci (i.e., common objectives). As the phrase "we as a people" suggests, the need for institutions is almost intuitive; ask anyone. Yet, the exact meaning of the term institution remains vague, obscure, often shrouded in mystery; the meaning and the significance seem just outside the grasp of Afrikan Americans.

Assessing Definitions of "Institution"
Definition promotes awareness; therefore, we must define terms such as institution and institutional infrastructure,

in the context of Afrikan American life as well as American society. We have already attempted to elucidate the connection between institutions, culture, and collective human actions. It is now time to put the term institution into a practical, rather than intellectual context. This definition process is important because it is a prerequisite to the muster of collective human action in the formation and maintenance of institutions.

We will move from the general to the specific, then focus on particular attributes of institutions as they relate to the condition and circumstance of Afrikan America. As you will see, the process of defining just what an institution is can be as simple or as complex as we choose. However, as it relates to this discussion, the definition of institution will tend toward the complex; the purpose of this exercise is to make that complexity manageable.

The American Heritage Dictionary of the English Language defines institution as "A relationship or behavioral pattern of importance in the life of a community or society."

According to Douglass C. North, author of *Institutions, Institutional Change and Economic Performance,*

> Institutions are the rules of the game in a society or, more formally, are the humanly devised constraints that shape human interaction. In consequence they structure incentives in human exchange, whether political, social, or economic.

Institutions are a higher order of organization. They are explicitly concerned with molding behavior. This theme is consistent with our view of culture as this higher order of organization is representative of the collective, rather than individual, aspect of culture. North continues:

Institutions reduce uncertainty by providing a structure to everyday life. They are a guide to human interaction, so that when we wish to greet friends on the street, drive an automobile, buy oranges, borrow money, form a business, bury our dead, or whatever, we know (or can learn easily) how to perform these tasks; institutions define and limit the set of choices of individuals. In the rest of this volume, institution will be used in the sense of legitimized social grouping. The institution in question may be a family, a game, or a ceremony. The legitimating authority may be personal, such as a father, doctor, judge, referee, or maître d'hotel. Or it may be diffused, for example, based by common assent on some general founding principle.

Here, the "brick and mortar" notion of institutions is dispelled in favor of a broader view. In a complex, "free" society, an individual may have too many choices. Institutions, when they are responsive, functional, and culturally connected to a people, relieve this burden. Again, Douglass North provides insight to the range of consideration when defining the term institution:

Institutions include any form of constraint that human beings devise to shape human interaction. Are institutions formal or informal? They can be either, and I am interested both in formal constraints - such as rules that human beings devise - and in informal constraints - such as conventions and codes of behavior. Institutions may be created, as was the United States Constitution; or they may simply evolve over time, as does common law.

These views of institution are from the vantage point of the dominant culture, which has a fully functional community. Are there more rudimentary, or basic, aspects to institutions that we have overlooked? These authors point out the role of institutions in the ordering of society and facilitating communication, cooperation, and coordination. They also point out that trust is a prerequisite to the formation of institutions.

All of these themes are relevant to the Afrikan American experience. While the dominant culture may view these issues as mundane, Afrikan Americans cannot. These are the issues we'll need to consider as we're building a community. Let us review:

- Institutions are rules or conventions.
- Institutions reduce uncertainty.
- Institutions can be formal or informal.
- Their scope can be narrow or broad.
- Institution may be public, private, or philanthropic.
- They may exist as local, state, national or global entities.
- Institutions free the individual of certain thinking-related tasks.

Institutions are critical to self-determination. If one's rules for living are imposed from outside one's culture, it is not self-determination.

If an institution is to be effective, it must have some method for translating law into action. There must be a mechanism to maintain, change, or modify behaviors. This implies an enforcement function, such as punishment and reward, on some level. Coercion, of various types and degrees, is a form of this mechanism. It could be argued, for example, that the edicts of the institution of the church are made manifest through moral suasion or coercion (i.e., the fear of going to hell).

Institutions and Organizations

Implicit in the idea of institutional enforcement is the voluntary submission of individual will and interests to the good of the collective as determined by the institution. This is only one attribute that sets institutions apart from "mere" organizations; there are others. North asserts his distinction between institutions and organizations as follows:

> Like institutions, organizations provide a structure to human interaction . . . .Conceptually, what must be clearly differentiated are the rules from the players. The purpose of the rules is to define the way the game is played. But the objective of the team within that set of rules is to win the game - by a combination of skills, strategy, and coordination; by fair means and sometimes by foul means.

Here, North is saying that the rules of the game (i.e., institutions, as rules for living) are separate and distinct from the players (i.e., individual people) or teams (i.e., organizations). The sports analogy is very instructive for Afrikan Americans; while we have individuals (players) and organizations (teams), we lack organization at the "league" (institutional) level. We have no league (community) of our own. North continues:

> Modeling the strategies and the skills of the team as it develops is a separate process from modeling the creation, evolution, and consequence of the rules.

This point is a particularly poignant one for those of us who would build, or modernize, an Afrikan American community. Afrikan American culture has not taken the evolutionary step necessary to recognize the very real process differences between organizations and institutions. There is a difference between institutions and organizations; an organization does not make an institution! Afrikan Americans have many organizations but few institutions.

We have already focused on the behavior molding and modifying functions of institutions. In the typical organization, this function is only implicit. Molding or modifying behavior is a chief function of institutions. This is typically not the case with mere organizations. As a vehicle for the expression of the collective will, Afrikan American institutions must assume the behavior molding function explicitly.

Organizations are generally expressions of individualism, in the sense that they represent relatively small and discrete constituencies; the same can be said for their missions and objectives. Institutions, on the other hand, tend to address the collective; they cast a wide net, embracing all or a substantial majority of a culture. Therefore, institutions represent a different *and* higher order of human interaction than do organizations.

The missing ingredients in Afrikan American life are a remembrance and acceptance of collective consciousness. A collective consciousness is present and operative in all distinct societies and cultures. A collective consciousness is a prerequisite to collective human actions toward shared cultural objectives. In America, collective human action is manifested through institutions. In the process of forgetting our collective consciousness, Afrikan Americans have lost sight of the importance of having our own institutions. While organizations and other forms of free association represent a level of collective human actions, their functions and scope are usually limited to a degree that they become expressions of individualism. Such organizations represent a lower order of human interactions than do institutions. To assist in assessing the state of Afrikan American institutions, an Institutional Status Worksheet (ISW) is provided. The ISW can be used to determine if an institution is functioning within the framework outlined in the text.

The issues in this book have concerned themselves with institutions. Institutions are viewed as a culture's primary mechanisms for shaping individual and collective behavior. Many organizations do this as well, but to a lesser extent or degree. We have suggested that there is a threshold level, in terms of functionality and scope as well as cultural orientation, that must be met in order to be considered a capable Afrikan American institution. A premise of this work is that Afrikan Americans are far too dependent on the institutions of the dominant culture and that we have far too few institutions of ours that are capable and fully devoted Afrikan American cultural objectives at the collective level. Our dependence on the institutions of the dominant culture is misplaced because those institutions are not responsive to the needs of Afrikan Americans. The proof, and the measure, of this non-responsiveness is the disparity that exists in American society between the dominant culture and Afrikan American culture.

Our cultural evolution in America has been under conditions of extreme duress. The duress of existing in America has *blinded* us to the mechanisms of collective human actions. That is to say, when is comes to a consideration of institutions, we go *unconscious*. If Afrikan

Americans are to wake up to our institutional *blindspot*, we must *consciously and deliberately* consider the role of institutions within the context of our culture and America's pluralistic society. The IWS capsulizes the logic and considerations for this conscious and deliberate process.

The Institutional Status Worksheet (ISW)

Generally speaking, we have described institutions as society's "rules for living"; we have stated that they are "mechanisms for collective human action." These are high order descriptions of institutions and may not convey the practical implications of how institutions operate, or not. The worksheet considers functionality, scope and cultural orientation, then examines the specific functions assigned to Afrikan American institutions within a given area of human activity. While both the functions of institutions and the areas of human activity are listed in a "stovepipe" manner in a matrix, the reader is alerted once again that all of the functions as well as the areas are interrelated and should not be viewed or considered in isolation. The ISW is a simple tool and can be used to determine how focused our institutions are. It can also be used to determine functional shortfalls that may exist within Afrikan American institutions.

The worksheet has three parts. Part I is a general assessment and decision tree that allows the user to determine if an entity or activity is an institution, based on the requirements of functionality and scope; this is the first "cut," or filter. If the entity or activity under consideration passes the first filter in Part I, it goes to the second filter, which is cultural orientation. This filter determines what culture the entity or activity supports. Part II of the ISW is a matrix which puts the assessment in an Afrikan American context; it examines the functions and the areas of human activity for Afrikan American institutions as proposed in the text. Part III is used to describe any observations relative to the assessment and to record the conclusions. Worksheets for the following entities/activities have been completed; these are subjective assessments conducted by the author:

> Public Schools
> U.S. Constitution
> Principles of Kwanzaa (Nguzo Saba)
> Black Entertainment Television (BET)
> The National Association for the Advancement
>   of Colored People (NAACP)
> Historically Black Colleges and
>   Universities (HBCUs)

Each of the above is considered to be "mechanisms for collective human action." They all mold or modulate individual and collective behavior and as such *may* qualify as institutions. Some of the institutions on the list are Afrikan American, some are dominant cultural institutions. Most importantly, the list is designed to explode the "brick and mortar" notion of institutions. Institutions are rules, or conventions, for living, irrespective of form. While the form of institutions may vary greatly, they are all mechanisms for collective human action The ISW provides a simplified method by which to make a determination and to analyze individual mechanism(s) under consideration. The ISW is a tool to assess individual (forms of) organization; it does not assess the overall institutional infrastructure.

INSTITUTIONAL STATUS WORKSHEET

NAME OF ENTITY: **PUBLIC SCHOOLS**

Part I - General Assessment

First Filter - Is it an institution?

Functionality: Does it mold, or seek to mold, collective behavior?
___ No (Stop! It is not an institution)
_X_ Yes (Go to Scope)

Scope: Does it impact, or seek to impact, the culture or a majority portion of the culture?

___ No (Stop! It is not an institution)
_X_ Yes (Go to Cultural Orientation)

Second Filter - Is it Afrikan American?

Cultural Orientation: What culture does it support, or seek to support?

__ It supports America's dominant culture (Stop; Part II does not apply)
_X_ It supports all cultures in America, but not equally (Pause; Part II is optional)
__It supports Afrikan American culture (Go to Part II)

Part II - Cultural Specific Assessment

Select the area or areas of human activity that best matches the entity or activity under consideration. Then place in "X" in all boxes that apply to that entity or activity. A "strong" Afrikan American institution would reflect an "X" in each function for a given area of human activity. A description of each function is found in Chapter 4 of the text.

Alternatively, the matrix may be used to "weight" or "score" an institution, relative to functions and areas of human activity. This is accomplished by assigning a value based on scale or range of values; this can be numerical, or other values.

AREAS OF HUMAN ACTIVITY
VERSUS
FUNCTIONS OF INSTITUTION

AREAS FUNCTIONS	WEALTH CREATION	HEALTH	EDUCATION	POLITICS, LAW AND JUSTICE	SECURITY AND DEFENSE	ENTERPRISE AND LIVELIHOOD	INTER-PERSONAL RELATION-SHIPS	ENTERTAINMENT, REST AND RELAXATION
KNOWLEDGE PRODUCTION			X					
VECTORS FOR BEHAVIOR			X					
COOR, COOP AND COMM			X					
DISCIPLINE AND DILIGENCE			X					
TEACHING AND LEARNING			X					
REPOSITORY			X					
WATCHDOG								
INNOVATION			X					

Part III - Observations and Conclusions

Schools are an institution. They are concerned with teaching and learning, with molding behavior consistent with an established curriculum. The public schools in America represent a democratic institution serving a majority of the nation. Public schools serve to provide a common experience for Americans and meld the various cultures around this common experience. And how can a nation endure without a common experience between and among it citizens? It can not. Public schools meet the institutional requirements of functionality and scope.

Yet public schools are but a reflection of the society, as a whole. On the score of cultural orientation we find that the schools are tilted toward the dominant culture. Its curriculums reflect dominant culture values in style and substance, considering other cultures only at the margins. Students are tested on their mastery of subject matter deemed important or necessary to the dominant culture. If a student is not of the dominant culture, it is difficult to see that he or she is a true stakeholder in American society. The curriculum reinforces and supports the cultural objectives of the dominant culture. These facts are not lost on our students. They sense, at the collective level, that the enterprise of American education does not really serve their (collective) interests. The basic incentive for learning (i.e., to assume one's rightful place in society) is thereby reduced. The joy of learning is diminished as well because an artificial incentive must arise as motivation. These artificial incentives include money, a "good" job, and/or status as conferred by the dominant culture. All of these things are merely modern day trinkets, if the student is not equipped with a strong sense of (the collective) Self. This sense of Self is what one's *own* institutions provide. The institutions of another can *never* provide this.

Carter G. Woodson aptly alerted us, so many years ago, that America's system of education fails on the criteria of cultural orientation. The disparity in "achievement" between Afrikan American children and those of the dominant culture is contrived and manufactured. It is more accurately a disparity in experience and resources. To remedy this does not require a retreat from the institution of public schools. But it does require an *institutional response* on our part. The disparity in "achievement" has as much to do with what happens outside of the classroom as within it. The disparity has to do with the *quality* of teaching and learning during "out of school" time. An appropriate institutional response may for example involve the establishment of a common cultural curriculum to be administered to our children during "out of school" time. Such an approach could be a part of existing "rites of passages" efforts that are working successfully in many Afrikan American communities. This is a way to "pick up the slack" where America's educational institutions have failed. The objective would be to bring *parity of experience* to our children and thereby a mastery of African and American cultures.

INSTITUTIONAL STATUS WORKSHEET

Part I - General Assessment

NAME OF ENTITY: **U.S. CONSTITUTION**

Part I - General Assessment

First Filter - Is it an institution?

      Functionality: Does it mold, or seek to mold, collective behavior?
         ___ No (Stop! It is not an institution)
         _X_ Yes (Go to Scope)

      Scope: Does it impact, or seek to impact, the culture or a majority portion of the culture?

         ___ No (Stop! It is not an institution)
         _X_ Yes (Go to Cultural Orientation)

Second Filter - Is it Afrikan American?

      Cultural Orientation: What culture does it support, or seek to support?

         ___ It supports America's dominant culture (Stop; Part II does not apply)
         _X_ It supports all cultures in America, but not equally (Pause; Part II is optional)
         ___ It supports Afrikan American culture (Go to Part II)

Part II - Cultural Specific Assessment

Select the area or areas of human activity that best matches the entity or activity under consideration. Then place in "X" in all boxes that apply to that entity or activity. A "strong" Afrikan American institution would reflect an "X" in each function for a given area of human activity. A description of each function is found in Chapter 4 of the text.

Alternatively, the matrix may be used to "weight" or "score" an institution, relative to functions and areas of human activity. This is accomplished by assigning a value based on scale or range of values; this can be numerical, or other values.

AREAS OF HUMAN ACTIVITY
VERSUS
FUNCTIONS OF INSTITUTION

AREAS ⟍ FUNCTIONS	WEALTH CREATION	HEALTH	EDUCATION	POLITICS, LAW AND JUSTICE	SECURITY AND DEFENSE	ENTERPRISE AND LIVELIHOOD	INTER-PERSONAL RELATION-SHIPS	ENTERTAINMENT, REST AND RELAXATION
KNOWLEDGE PRODUCTION	X	X	X	X	X	X	X	X
VECTORS FOR BEHAVIOR	X	X	X	X	X	X	X	X
COOR, COOP AND COMM	X	X	X	X	X	X	X	X
DISCIPLINE AND DILIGENCE	X	X	X	X	X	X	X	X
TEACHING AND LEARNING	X	X	X	X	X	X	X	X
REPOSITORY	X	X	X	X	X	X	X	X
WATCHDOG	X	X	X	X	X	X	X	X
INNOVATION	X	X	X	X	X	X	X	X

Part III - Observations and Conclusions

The U.S. Constitution is a meta institution which forms the foundation for the governance of the nation. A vast array of lesser (or enabling) institutions and other forms of free association now exist in support of the Constitution. This vast array is the institutional infrastructure of the United States. It is the totality of all institutions that work toward the cultural objectives of America's dominant culture. In theory, the Constitution is applicable to all cultures of this plural society. In practice it is a device that can be manipulated, contorted, even ignored at the whims and biases of the dominant culture. In fashioning a democracy, the nation's founders recognized that political, religious, and cultural minorities would require "protection" against the tyranny of the majority. The Constitution contemplates goodwill, which is the currency of culture. The Constitution did not contemplate the rise of a global system of racism/white supremacy, which is hatred, the complete absence of goodwill.

The formation of institutions in response to the guiding principles of the Constitution is a logical consequence of freedom (of association). The denial of freedom, in this context, is both illogical and irrational. The denial of freedom, in various and multiple forms, imposed on Black citizens accounts for the present day disparate situation of Afrikan Americans. The formation of this country and the evolution of its institutional infrastructure should be instructive for us.

The Afrikan in America has challenged the precepts of the Constitution, making reality out of ideals. Imbued with Spirit, Afrikan Americans have been the test of the (Constitutional) metal. Even when a majority of Americans

76

have been slow or reluctant to live up to the ideals, Afrikan Americans have proved to be the consciousness of the nation, the Spirit of America.

INSTITUTIONAL STATUS WORKSHEET

NAME OF ENTITY: **PRINCIPLES OF KWANZAA, NGUZO SABA**

Part I - General Assessment-

First Filter - Is it an institution?

    Functionality: Does it mold or seek to mold behavior?

        ___ No (Stop! It is not an institution)

        _X_ Yes (Go to Scope)

    Scope: Does it impact or seek to impact the culture or a majority portion of the culture?

        ___ No (Stop! It is not an institution)

        _X_ Yes (Go to Cultural Orientation)

Second Filter - Is it Afrikan American?

    Cultural Orientation: What cultural objectives does it support, or seek to support?

        ___ It supports America's dominant culture (Stop; Part II does not apply)

        ___ It supports all cultures in America, but not equally (Pause; Part II is optional)

        _X_ It supports Afrikan American culture (Go to Part II)

Part II - Cultural Specific Assessment

Select the area or areas of human activity that best matches the entity or activity under consideration. Then place in "X" in all boxes that apply to that entity or activity. A "strong" Afrikan American institution would reflect an "X" in each function for a given area of human activity. A description of each function is found in Chapter 4 of the text.

Alternatively, the matrix may be used to "weight" or "score" an institution, relative to functions and areas of human activity. This is accomplished by assigning a value based on scale or range of values; this can be numerical, or other values.

AREAS OF HUMAN ACTIVITY
VERSUS
FUNCTIONS OF INSTITUTION

AREAS FUNCTIONS	WEALTH CREATION	HEALTH	EDUCATION	POLITICS, LAW AND JUSTICE	SECURITY AND DEFENSE	ENTERPRISE AND LIVELIHOOD	INTER-PERSONAL RELATION-SHIPS	ENTERTAINMENT, REST AND RELAXATION
PRODUCTION KNOWLEDGE	X	X	X	X	X	X	X	X
VECTORS FOR BEHAVIOR	X	X	X	X	X	X	X	X
COOR, COOP AND COMM	X	X	X	X	X	X	X	X
DISCIPLINE AND DILIGENCE	X	X	X	X	X	X	X	X
TEACHING AND LEARNING	X	X	X	X	X	X	X	X
REPOSITORY								
WATCHDOG								
INNOVATION								

Part III - Observations and Conclusions: The Principles of Kwanzaa, formally referred to as the Nguzo Saba, represent a meta-institution. While an institution usually specializes in a *subset* of an area of human activity, meta institutions are at once, general and pervasive. They tend to impact *all or several* areas of human activity. The Nguzo Saba seeks to mold individual and collective behavior toward an Afrocentric ideal. In this regard, the Nguzo Saba is a broad based construct, impacting all of the areas of human activity. The Nguzo Saba represents a meta-institution in the same sense as say, the U.S. Constitution and, as the Constitution, these important principles require the development of an array of lesser (or enabling) institutions and other foundations in their support, if they are to endure in an American context.

The Nguzo Saba, or Seven Principles of the Black Value System, takes a more direct route to the collective consciousness than do the more "conventional" institutions (i.e., institutions in a form suitable to the dominant culture). The Nguzo Saba takes a form that is consistent with our African past, that is, customs, traditions, and rituals. The celebration of Kwanzaa provides a mechanism and opportunity for the expression of principle into action.

The Principles of Kwanzaa are said to flow from the Kawaida Theory which is an African-derived thought style based on tradition and reason. It is estimated that some ten million people observe the Kwanzaa celebration each year from December 26 through January 1. The widespread acceptance and adoption of Kwanzaa affords sufficient scope to consider the Nguzo Saba as an institution.

Part II of the assessment shows that the Seven Principles of the Black Value System are all-encompassing in terms of providing vectors for behavior (and human actions). However, in term of the functional architecture for institutions as described in the text (i.e., what institutions should do), the Nguzo Saba lacks the institutional underpinnings necessary for maximum cultural impact and sustainment. To be truly effective, institutions that would promulgate the Seven Principles must do all eight functions required of institutions. The functions of repository, watchdog, and innovation are not dispensable. The provisions for these functions are not evident in the overall construct for the Nguzo Saba (nor are they explicitly excluded). These functions are very much necessary for the maintenance and perpetuation of culture.

In other words, we need to expand and extend the practice of the Nguzo Saba beyond the narrow confines of the Kwanzaa celebration. The Nguzo Saba needs to evolve beyond a family and/or community endeavor (these are essentially manifestations of *individualism*). Rather, all Afrikan American organizations should seek to imbue themselves with the more potent *collective* aspects of this system of thought (and actions). This would require that organizations seek to incorporate, integrate, and/or affirm the Seven Principles of the Black Value System into their (operational) way of life. It is not enough to maintain the relatively low level of active participation in the Nguzo Saba (i.e., when viewed from a year round perspective), these things must be practiced, refined, cultivated, supported, and propagated on a daily basis.

The Nguzo Saba explodes the myths of institutions as "bricks and mortar"; these principles demonstrate in a dramatic and relevant way, how and why institutions are "rules for living." In a sense, the overarching nature of the Nguzo Saba suggests that the present method of assessment should be subservient to it. That is to say, the Seven Principles represent a path to collective consciousness in their own right. Yet an outstanding question still remains and that question is, what is the mechanism for achieving or realizing that consciousness? This leads us back to institutions! Institutions are the outward manifestation of the consciousness that is raised by the Nguzo Saba. The seeds of the Nguzo Saba have been planted in the consciousness of Afrikan America and this is fertile ground. If the seed is good (as determined by the collective consciousness), then we anticipate a great harvest. In the meantime, the crop must be tended. That is the role of institutions, culture's mechanism for collective human action.

INSTITUTIONAL STATUS WORKSHEET

NAME OF ENTITY: **BLACK ENTERTAINMENT TELEVISION, INC.**

Part I - General Assessment-

First Filter - Is it an institution?

> **Functionality**: Does it mold or seek to mold behavior?
> > ___No (Stop! It is not an institution)
> > _X Yes (Go to Scope)

> **Scope**: Does it impact or seek to impact the culture or a majority portion of the culture?

> > ___No (Stop! It is not an institution)
> > _X Yes (Go to Cultural Orientation)

Second Filter - Is it Afrikan American?

> **Cultural Orientation**: What cultural objectives does it support, or seek to support?

> > ___It supports America's dominant culture (Stop; Part II does not apply)
> > _X_ It supports all cultures in America, but not equally (Pause; Part II is optional)
> > ___It supports Afrikan American culture (Go to Part II)

Part II - Cultural Specific Assessment

Select the area or areas of human activity that best matches the entity or activity under consideration. Then place in "X" in all boxes that apply to that entity or activity. A "strong" Afrikan American institution would reflect an

"X" in each function for a given area of human activity. A description of each function is found in Chapter 4 of the text.

Alternatively, the matrix may be used to "weight" or "score" an institution, relative to functions and areas of human activity. This is accomplished by assigning a value based on scale or range of values; this can be numerical, or other values.

AREAS OF HUMAN ACTIVITY
VERSUS
FUNCTIONS OF INSTITUTION

AREAS / FUNCTIONS	WEALTH CREATION	HEALTH	EDUCATION	POLITICS, LAW AND JUSTICE	SECURITY AND DEFENSE	ENTERPRISE AND LIVELIHOOD	INTER-PERSONAL RELATION-SHIPS	ENTERTAINMENT, REST AND RELAXATION
KNOWLEDGE PRODUCTION						X		
VECTORS FOR BEHAVIOR						X		
COOR, COOP AND COMM						X		
DISCIPLINE AND DILIGENCE						X		
TEACHING AND LEARNING						X		
REPOSITORY	X					X		X
WATCHDOG								
INNOVATION								

Part III - Observations and Conclusions

Black Entertainment Television, Inc., is a corporation. Corporations are narrowly focused institutions concerned with the objective of prosperity (or in the case of the dominant culture, greed). Corporations mold the behavior of its members, clients, and/or customers; in this sense they are mechanisms of collectivism. In terms of the areas of human activity, corporations are best described as enterprises, or businesses. Businesses, of course, operate in all areas of human activity, including leisure (entertainment, rest and relaxation). Corporations can be multinational, thus extend their scope and sphere of influence to global dimensions.

BET, and any other corporation, represents a "special case," or particular kind of institution. The rules governing the legal establishment of corporations assign to them the characteristics of a person. By so doing, these mechanisms of collectivism are "transformed" into individuals, by law and in the eyes of the courts. The corporation has a persona and legal standing of its own, separate and distinct from the owners and operators of the corporation. In such an arrangement, accountability is not easily fixed. Corporations are free floating institutional entities (some would even say, life forms!) wielding tremendous influence and power over society, without any real checks or balances over their activities other than "the market." Corporations are a dominant culture invention providing a mechanism to achieve the collective cultural objective of prosperity (and greed). For corporations to serve any other purpose would require a conscious, deliberate, and concerted effort.

In America, most corporations are formed under the institutional framework of the dominant culture. As such they are, by default, working toward cultural objectives of the dominant culture. Those objectives are racism/white supremacy and greed. BET is no exception. Is BET an Afrikan American institution? Bob Johnson illustrated this when he sold it to Viacom. Many Afrikan American businesses want Black consumers to support them because they are Afrikan American, while they will sell it in a heartbeat to the highest White bidder. There is nothing African about BET, neither Continental nor Diasporian. BET is "all American." BET's programming, or content, is driven by the bottom line and is divorced completely from considerations of (African or Afrikan American) culture. BET reflects the popular culture; this "pop" culture is highly commercial and ephemeral. The pop culture is driven by the profit motive. BET provides a media outlet for Afrikan American contributions to the pop culture and it is positioned to provide access to all (people). The sad fact is that without an Afrikan American institutional infrastructure, the *individual* Afrikan American business (wo)man has no option but capitulation to the dominant culture's system of capitalism. Given this reality, the usual response of the Black business (wo)man is to either distance one's self from the community or engage in some "give back to the community" fantasy as a balm.

Most Afrikan American businesses are American at the core and African at the margins, if at all. We must seek to flip this script. At the core, our corporations and other business endeavors must reflect our cultural striving, which are African by definition. An environment of pluralism demands this. Prosperity (and/or greed) can be satisfied at the margins, with plenty left over. Corporations, like much of American society, represent a paradox. They are at once, expressions of individualism (as prescribed by law) and to a lesser extent, mechanisms of collective human action. The problem for Afrikan Americans is that the profit motive is individualist in its manifestation and tends to push the realization of collective consciousness from remembrance. For a culture whose collective nature is fully manifested in a functional institutional infrastructure such as America's dominant culture, this may be acceptable behavior. But for a culture with an unmanifested sense of the collective consciousness, such behavior is detrimental.

Institutions Build Strong Communities

INSTITUTIONAL STATUS WORKSHEET

NAME OF ENTITY: **NATIONAL ASSOCIATION FOR THE ADVANCEMENT OF COLORED PEOPLE (NAACP)**

Part I - General Assessment-

First Filter - Is it an institution?

    Functionality: Does it mold or seek to mold behavior?
        ___No (Stop! It is not an institution)
        _X_ Yes (Go to Scope)

    Scope: Does it impact or seek to impact the culture or a majority portion of the culture?

        ___No (Stop! It is not an institution)
        _X_ Yes (Go to Cultural Orientation)

Second Filter - Is it Afrikan American?

    Cultural Orientation: What cultural objectives does it support, or seek to support?

        ___It supports America's dominant culture (Stop; Part II does not apply)
        _X_ It supports all cultures in America, but not equally (Pause; Part II is optional)
        ___It supports Afrikan American culture (Go to Part II)

Part II - Cultural Specific Assessment

Select the area or areas of human activity that best matches the entity or activity under consideration. Then place in "X" in all boxes that apply to that entity or activity. A "strong" Afrikan American institution would reflect an "X" in each function for a given area of human activity. A description of each function is found in Chapter 4 of the text.

Alternatively, the matrix may be used to "weight" or "score" an institution, relative to functions and areas of human activity. This is accomplished by assigning a value based on scale or range of values; this can be numerical, or other values.

AREAS OF HUMAN ACTIVITY
VERSUS
FUNCTIONS OF INSTITUTION

AREAS / FUNCTIONS	WEALTH CREATION	HEALTH	EDUCATION	POLITICS, LAW AND JUSTICE	SECURITY AND DEFENSE	ENTERPRISE AND LIVELIHOOD	INTER-PERSONAL RELATION-SHIPS	ENTERTAINMENT, REST AND RELAXATION
KNOWLEDGE PRODUCTION				X				
VECTORS FOR BEHAVIOR				X				
COOR, COOP AND COMM				X				
DISCIPLINE AND DILIGENCE				X				
TEACHING AND LEARNING				X				
REPOSITORY				X				
WATCHDOG	X	X	X	X	X	X		X
INNOVATION								

Part III - Observations and Conclusions

The NAACP is considered by some to be the pre-
miere Afrikan American organization. Is the NAACP an
Afrikan American institution or merely an organization?
How does it stack up, in terms of function, scope, and cultural orientation?

The NAACP is a civil rights organization; it operates
within the institutional climate of the nation's political,
legal, and justice systems and institutions. It is an organization that looks outward and seeks to affect civil rights-
related change within dominant culture institutions. It
seeks to mold *their* behavior. On this basis it meets the
functionality requirement. While the NAACP professes

to operate on behalf of all "colored" people, its actual membership rolls include only a small percentage of the Afrikan American population. Historically, the impact of the NAACP has been more broad than its membership rolls would suggest. While one may differ with its focus and direction, the NAACP has sufficient scope to bring it to the level of institution.

The issue of cultural orientation presents a challenge for the NAACP (and most other Black organizations as well). Because of its integrationist leanings, the NAACP works in subtle ways to undermine collective consciousness within the Afrikan American community. Integration is about becoming a part of another's culture and in the case of Afrikan Americans, this would be done at the expense of our own culture. This fact has been demonstrated over the last fifty years. The more we have persued integration, the more our own institutions have fallen into disarray. Simply put, the NAACP was established and has evolved within the institutional framework of the dominant culture. It is a very formidable organization with the narrow focus of civil rights. While the NAACP may be an institution, its cultural orientation is dubious. Its ascendence to institutional status with the context of Afrikan American culture is predicated on its ability to garner the trust of a majority of Afrikan Americans and to update its agenda such that it is relevant to Afrikan American cultural objectives and values. As an Afrikan American institution, the NAACP should be concerned chiefly with molding our behavior; it should look at its internal mission with the same zeal as its external activities. Institutions and culture are interrelated. It is this relationship that makes institutions an imperative for cultural development. Therefore, institutions are connected in a very fundamental way to the culture(s) (and people) they support. Organizations may contribute to cultural development as well, but using the sports analogy, organizations are players or teams operating within established rules; they do not set the rules. Institutions set the rules for living. Given its integrationist views, the NAACP is a dominant culture institution.

INSTITUTIONAL STATUS WORKSHEET

NAME OF ENTITY: **HISTORICALLY BLACK COLLEGES AND UNIVERSITIES (HBCUs)**

Part I - General Assessment-

First Filter - Is it an institution?

> **Functionality**: Does it mold or seek to mold behavior?
> ___No (Stop! It is not an institution)
> _X Yes (Go to Scope)

> **Scope**: Does it impact or seek to impact the culture or a majority portion of the culture?
>
> > ___No (Stop! It is not an institution)
> > _X Yes (Go to Cultural Orientation)

Second Filter - Is it Afrikan American?

> **Cultural Orientation**: What cultural objectives does it support, or seek to support?
>
> > ___It supports America's dominant culture (Stop; Part II does not apply)
> > _X It supports all cultures in America, but not equally (Pause; Part II is optional)
> > ___It supports Afrikan American culture (Go to Part II)

Part II - Cultural Specific Assessment

Select the area or areas of human activity that best matches the entity or activity under consideration. Then place in "X" in all boxes that apply to that entity or activity. A "strong" Afrikan American institution would reflect an "X" in each function for a given area of human activity. A description of each function is found in Chapter 4 of the text.

Alternatively, the matrix may be used to "weight" or "score" an institution, relative to functions and areas of human activity. This is accomplished by assigning a value based on scale or range of values; this can be numerical, or other values.

AREAS OF HUMAN ACTIVITY
VERSUS
FUNCTIONS OF INSTITUTION

AREAS / FUNCTIONS	WEALTH CREATION	HEALTH	EDUCATION	POLITICS, LAW AND JUSTICE	SECURITY AND DEFENSE	ENTERPRISE AND LIVELIHOOD	INTER-PERSONAL RELATION-SHIPS	ENTERTAINMENT, REST AND RELAXATION
KNOWLEDGE PRODUCTION	X	X	X	X		X	X	X
VECTORS FOR BEHAVIOR	X	X	X	X		X	X	X
COOR, COOP AND COMM	X	X	X	X		X	X	X
DISCIPLINE AND DILIGENCE	X	X	X	X		X	X	X
TEACHING AND LEARNING	X	X	X	X		X	X	X
REPOSITORY	X	X	X	X		X	X	X
WATCHDOG								
INNOVATION	X	X	X	X		X	X	X

These existing institutions have the necessary *breadth* to encompass and capture our knowledge system and attendant essential information. As an example individual universities could become "centers of excellence" for each of the eight areas of human activity and serve as the focal point around which existing organizations and communities could coalesce in support of cultural objectives.

INSTITUTIONAL STATUS WORKSHEET

NAME OF ENTITY: _____

Part I - General Assessment-

First Filter - Is it an institution?

    Functionality: Does it mold or seek to mold behavior?
        ___No (Stop! It is not an institution)
        ___Yes (Go to Scope)

    Scope: Does it impact or seek to impact the culture or a majority portion of the culture?

        ___No (Stop! It is not an institution)
        ___Yes (Go to Cultural Orientation)

Second Filter - Is it Afrikan American?

    Cultural Orientation: What cultural objectives does it support, or seek to support?

        ___It supports America's dominant culture (Stop; Part II does not apply)
        ___It supports all cultures in America, but not equally (Pause; Part II is optional)
        ___It supports Afrikan American culture (Go to Part II)

Part II - Cultural Specific Assessment

Select the area or areas of human activity that best matches the entity or activity under consideration. Then place in "X" in all boxes that apply to that entity or activity. A "strong" Afrikan American institution would reflect an "X" in each function for a given area of human activity. A description of each function is found in Chapter 4 of the text.

Alternatively, the matrix may be used to "weight" or "score" an institution, relative to functions and areas of human activity. This is accomplished by assigning a value based on scale or range of values; this can be numerical, or other values.

AREAS OF HUMAN ACTIVITY
VERSUS
FUNCTIONS OF INSTITUTION

AREAS / FUNCTIONS	WEALTH CREATION	HEALTH	EDUCATION	POLITICS, LAW AND JUSTICE	SECURITY AND DEFENSE	ENTERPRISE AND LIVELIHOOD	INTER-PERSONAL RELATION-SHIPS	ENTERTAINMENT, REST AND RELAXATION
KNOWLEDGE PRODUCTION								
VECTORS FOR BEHAVIOR								
COOR, COOP AND COMM								
DISCIPLINE AND DILIGENCE								
TEACHING AND LEARNING								
REPOSITORY								
WATCHDOG								
INNOVATION								

Part III - Observations and Conclusions

The issue of cultural orientation has enormous and ominous implications for Afrikan American culture. If an infrastructure is not viable, then our institutions and organizations actually exist within the institutional climate of the dominant culture. In many cases, what we have is the organizational corollary to the Black Anglo-Saxon. Black

Anglo Saxon makes reference to Nathan Hare's classic, critical analysis of racism's manifestations in Black people (self-hatred). In the absence of an African or Afrikan American community, our organizations (as well as individuals and institutions) are by default working toward the cultural objectives of the dominant culture; those objectives are racism/white supremacy and greed. This is at once an indictment and an appeal to wake up. Another contemporary effect of the Black Anglo-Saxon syndrome is that much of the Afrikan American intellectual brain power is co-opted by the corporate and governmental institutions of the dominant culture. While the cumulative effect of these *individual* defections may diminish our overall numbers, in no way does it impact our power or potential at the collective level. It is my optimistic view that given a strong Afrikan American community, those who are now co-opted will return in support and defense of the African culture in America.

It is communities which give power, direction, and meaning to the activities of individuals, organizations, and institutions. An institution meets the cultural orientation criteria if it seeks to change the consciousness and behaviors of Afrikan Americans. Clearly, this is different from the orientation of the dominant culture which is the racism/white supremacy and greed.

The cultural orientation of Afrikan American institutions must be afrocentric. Author and scholar Molefi Asante has done an excellent job of defining afrocentricity. We must view the world from an African frame of reference. We must apply the values of the Nguzo Saba.

Institutions include schools, churches, courts, family, the Constitution, and corporations. We can see how these mold and modulate individual and collective behaviors. Other institutions operate more covertly and have hidden agendas. To determine if an institution meets our needs, question its function (i.e., does the entity mold or modulate behavior?), scope (i.e., does it impact the culture broadly?), and cultural orientation (i.e., what culture or cultures does the institution or organization support?).

The Relationship between Institutions and Culture

Cultures are sustained or maintained through institutions. This is *why* institutions are so very important. What is culture? We have previously stated that culture is simply how individuals and groups get along with one another. This simple definition of culture is important because (1) it implies the need for the races to get along, (2) it embodies the cultural objectives of survival and prosperity, and (3) it seeks to address the persistent effects of the maafa.

In the atmosphere of American apartheid known as segregation, Afrikan Americans established their own infrastructure of institutions that co-existed with the infrastructure of America's White culture. This was achieved naturally and in due course. While the interference from Whites was a detriment, this arrangement did allow for more functionality of the infrastructure than we have now. Ironically, segregation helped keep the Afrikan American community together. If integration was to be pursued, we should have taken care to maintain our institutions. We apparently assumed that the institutions of the dominant culture would somehow be responsive to our needs. That did not happen.

Community

Is society working? This is where the idea of community enters. Community is concerned with how groups of people (cultures) survive and prosper. Community is the totality (breadth and depth) of the institutions of a people; it includes all institutions supporting a particular culture.

Homogeneous cultures tend toward a single community. Pluralistic societies, such as America, tend toward multiple communities. The more viable the community, the more successful are the people it supports.

America is an imperfect pluralistic society. A pluralistic society has many groups (political, ethnic, cultural) and power issues (economic, political, moral, etc.). In a truly pluralistic society, these groups compete with each other as they vie for society's resources. America's pluralistic society is imperfect and flawed because it has a dominant culture that controls the lion's share of power and wealth, mostly ill-gotten gains. America's dominant culture is White and pathologically anti-Black. This group controls the principal community in America. The story of the emergence of America's institutions was chronicled by French author Alexis de Tocqueville more than one hundred and fifty years ago.

We all depend on the principal community. It is what we all have in common with the dominant culture. The principal community belongs to all Americans; all have contributed, directly and indirectly, to its establishment and maintenance. Yet, community is only responsive to the needs of others to the extent that their conditions and circumstance are the same as that of the dominant culture. Indeed, groups other than the dominant culture have found it necessary to establish communities of their own to accomplish the following objectives:

(1) to negotiate with or to influence the principal infra structure of the nation and

(2) to "pick up the slack" when the dominant culture's infrastructure fails to meet needs.

These two objectives highlight the dilemma of numerical minorities (Afrikan Americans) in America. How does a minority influence or change the thinking and behaviors of America's institutions (i.e., white supremacy)? As previously stated, even if the interests of Afrikan Americans were highly defined (they are not) and agreed to by Black people (they are not), we do not have the *numbers* to be properly represented in America's institutions or to change them. Simultaneously, dominant culture institutions impact us with life and death issues. Not only do American institutions fail to meet our needs, they are not properly policed to ensure that their activities do not hurt us.

We Afrikan Americans traded our birthright for the promise of American institutions coming to our rescue through integration. That did not happen, as can be measured by the great disparity present between Afrikan Americans and the dominant culture. Disparity takes on an even more grotesque dimension as we examine health, education, politics, law, justice, enterprise (business) and livelihood (jobs), security and defense, etc. More than one hundred and thirty years after slavery, the need for collective human actions by Afrikan Americans is obvious. Such collective actions can be undertaken and sustained *only* through institutions.

Institutional continuity is more applicable to voluntary emigrants and less applicable to Afrikan Americans due to our slave past. This is so because the institutions and culture of the African slave (i.e., customs, rituals, traditions) came under vicious and continuous attack, ostensibly in the interest of control and domination. To America, emigrants were able to bring with them their culture and institutions. They were also able to maintain their relationships with each other and maintain the relationship of the individual to the collective. Slaves were not afforded this basic and essential human right. In fact, the dominant culture (with State complicity) did everything humanly possible to stamp out vestiges of African culture institutions in the slave population.

Without a fully functional community, the assertion *"we as a people"* rings hollow. Disenfranchisement results, including poverty amid opulence. Pathologies also result, including voter apathy, fatherlessness, rampant crime and violence, and a myriad of social and economic attacks on our community by outsiders. Black people recognize the lack of depth in our organizational structure. We respond by trying to escape and refusing to participate. Community conveys identity and purpose for living. The community is concerned with strategic thinking, freeing the individual to concentrate on the tactics of living.

Lack of a viable community is the determinant factor of the quality of life for Afrikan Americans. We must equip ourselves with the essential information of the meaning and roles of institutions in America and the world, then move in a deliberate way to build a fully functional institutional infrastructure. We must achieve and move from Ghetto to Community in all walks of life.

Institutions, Information, and the Production of Knowledge
Institutions (1) manage information, (2) produce knowledge, and (3) apply knowledge to the betterment of the human condition. This requires a knowledge system or thought style. Taking a macro-cultural view, such a system embodies the information and knowledge necessary for the survival and prosperity of a people. Groups of people have distinct knowledge systems; some are highly organized, some are not. The survival and prosperity of a people are dependent on (1) having essential information, (2) having a context for that information, (3) having a

mechanism for the conversion of that information into useful human knowledge (knowledge production), and finally (4) the ability to apply that knowledge as sustained human action. These are the elements that comprise the knowledge system. In describing the relationship of institutions to the knowledge system, institutions are the clogs, the gears, and the wheels of the knowledge system; they are the knowledge system made manifest.

In the post civil rights era, Afrikan Americans have attempted to piggyback on the knowledge system (and thereby, the institutional infrastructure) of the dominant culture in America. A certain amount of piggybacking is justified since we do have a stake in the principal community and the common knowledge system. However, we must understand that the dominant culture's knowledge system and infrastructure are responsive first to the dominant culture and to others only second, if at all.

We must bear in mind that the community of the dominant culture exerts an enormous influence over us as individuals and as a collective. Mary Douglas comments:

> The individual within the collective is never, or hardly ever, conscious of the prevailing thought style which almost always exerts an absolutely compulsive force upon his thinking, and with which it is not possible to be at variance.

The influence of the dominant culture can present a formidable barrier to the formation of an effective Afrikan American community. Interference should be anticipated and resisted. Dominant culture is seductive, and it attracts the Afrikan American (wo)man within its compulsive force. This is what Carter G. Woodson called the miseducation of the Negro. It devalues Black worth and potential.

As Afrikan Americans, our task is to gain access to and manage the information that is essential to us. We possess a unique body of knowledge that the world needs. This body of knowledge is our knowledge system and the basis of our culture and community. Individuals have only so much information processing power. With today's information overload, the individual cannot possibly keep track of and remain responsive to all the information impacting his survival and prosperity. For practical and psychological reasons, it is necessary for the individual to hand over certain responsibilities to the mechanisms of collectivism. These responsibilities include, but are not limited to, information gathering and processing. Such a delegation of responsibility is justified by the concept of division of labor. Mary Douglas makes the following point:

> A comforting but false idea about institutional thinking has gained some recent currency. This is the notion that institutions just do routine, low-level, day-to-day thinking. Andrew Schotter, who has so well described institutions as machines for thinking, believes that the minor decisions get off-loaded for institutional processing, while the mind of the individual is left free to weigh jimportant and difficult matters." (Schotter 1981, p. 149) There is no reason to believe in any such benign dispensation. The contrary is more likely to prevail. The individual tends to leave the important decisions to his institutions while busying himself with tactics and details.

In other words, institutions handle the really important collective decisions in our lives, including life and death decisions. Institutions help us do other things, as well.

Coordination, cooperation, and communication, which will be called the "three C's," are the essence of discourse in a civil society. Each of the three C's implies interaction of two or more individuals; they are, therefore, within the providence of the collective. Institutions can facilitate the three C's, as long as there is trust between individuals, institutions, and community. Trust is an issue because of maafa. Imagine, for hundreds of years an oppression so great that a man could not protect his wife or family from being violated by some wretched individual, nor prevent his family from being sold or otherwise split up at the whim of some slave owner. Imagine hundreds of years where favorites are conferred based on the lightness of skin or a myriad of other physical or psychological devices used to divide and conquer. Such conditions did not enhance trust between Black men and women.

There have been no attempts by the perpetrators of the atrocity to repair the damage, nor have we attempted to heal our interpersonal relationships. In fact, members of the dominant culture have continued to exploit this fissure. A lack of trust negatively impacts our ability to coordinate, cooperate, and communicate effectively within our own group.

Interestingly, the three C's form the basis for individual and collective economic activity. Economic activity is about relationships. Within the Afrikan American community, our economic effectiveness is reduced because of the lack of trust we have for one another. Our collective participation and performance in the American economy would suggest that we have more trust in our captors than we do in each other; we have been conditioned to think that way.

Institutions represent a way out the quagmire of damaged interpersonal relationships as they are, by definition, concerned with coordination, cooperation, and communication. Institutions can facilitate trust among people.

Context of information contributes to the three "C's," particularly communication. The context of information determines its usefulness; conversely, information without context is useless, at best. In *Beyond Culture*, Edward T. Hall states:

> The level of context determines everything about communication and is the foundation on which all subsequent behavior rests (including symbolic behavior).

Institutions provide the lens through which we view the world. They also provide structure and predictability. Each of these attributes aids the individual; yet, at the level of the collective, institutions work quite independently and perhaps more covertly than do individual members of society.

Context lends meaning to the cultural framework. Context is where we as a people are coming from. Without context, we have no way to determine the relative worth or merit of information. Within the field of economics, he who holds the most relevant information holds the advantage in the transaction. This condition, and the uncertainty associated with it, highlights the importance of information in economics. At a macro-cultural level, institutions become the mechanism for the regulation of information.

The Functions of Afrikan American Institutions

Institutions are a manifestation of collective consciousness, first and foremost. They lend expression to this consciousness. Institutions are required to maintain and perpetuate a culture. If we are required to build institutions in support of Afrikan American culture, to what specification would we build them? The specifications of our institutions and communities should be informed by our collective consciousness since consciousness precedes institutions development.

It is possible to specify the function of an institution without knowing the form it might take. No single individual can determine the form that a culture's institutions should take. As we examine and assess the internal and external cultural environment of Afrikan Americans, we can propose a list of functions to which our institutions must adhere. These functions would have an immediate and lasting impact on the lives of Afrikan Americans.

The following list of functions can serve as a template for designing an institution. While the institutions that support America's dominant culture have specific forms, we are not locked into those forms.

1. **Engaged in Knowledge Production.**
2. **Behavior Surveyors.**
3. **Agents for Coordination, Cooperation, and Communication.**
4. **Source for Societal Discipline and Diligence.**
5. **Engaged in Teaching and Learning.**
6. **Repositories of Knowledge and Information.**
7. **Engaged in a Watchdog Function**
8. **Catalyst for Innovation.**

The Functions of Afrikan American Institutions

The functions listed are really standards. Failure to meet one or more of these standards would relegate a would-be institution to mere organizational status. These are the essential functions that must be exercised by Afrikan American institutions to resolve the many disparities caused by America's dominant cultural institutions.

1. Knowledge Production. To what extent does the entity engage in knowledge production that supports the Afrikan American community? The production of human knowledge and its importance to society is not very well understood within the general population. As applied to Afrikan American institutions, knowledge production involves the conversion of information and data into forms that are useful to members of society. For example, research is a product of the knowledge function of colleges and universities. Knowledge is also produced by government agencies, businesses and industry, think tanks, the military intelligence community, social service agencies, etc.

Technology is a by-product of knowledge production. Technology is the application of human knowledge. First is the research function. When knowledge is produced, applications are developed based on what was discovered.

Afrikan American cultural beliefs say that technological applications of knowledge are merely objects of consumption. Such a belief misses the point and purpose of technology. The technology that we produce is indicative of the care, consideration, and importance that we attach to our knowledge system. It is also indicative of the degree to which we are engaged in the business of knowledge production. The problem is that we are contributors to the dominant cultures' knowledge system, but it is not our own. This fact is reflected in the nature of the technologies produced and to whom the benefits flow. Most Americans benefit from various technologies, but the wealth goes only to a few in the dominant culture.

Indeed, the dominant culture's preoccupation and enchantment with technology suggest that there is a greater psychological purpose. Technology seems to be a substitute for something that is lacking within the culture. Is technology a substitute for consciousness, spirit, soul, or even God? If this is the case, then technology is a poor and inadequate substitute. Every technology has a down side that is at least equal to its benefits. We may choose not to recognize or identify the down side to particular technologies, but it is nevertheless there.

Afrikan Americans must rethink our basic relationship to and understanding of technology and its role in society. We do not substitute technology for spirit, so we can put it in perspective and use it to benefit our community. Technology may be used to extinguish many disparities, thus moving us from ghetto to community. We must close the digital divide. Every Afrikan American must become computer literate and have access to the Internet. Through technology, we have the ability to communicate simultaneously with 40 million Afrikan Americans, 200 million Afrikans in central and south America and 800 million Afrikans on the continent, plus our people in other parts of the world. We can build community over the Internet.

2. Behavior Surveyors. Institutions modulate behavior in various ways; they lay before us the behavioral paths we should follow. We have mentioned that conventions, rituals, ceremony, and rules are facilitated by institutions. These are behavioral paths; Afrikan American institutions must establish behavioral protocols for individuals. Given the myth of the primacy of the individual, this may seem like a tall order for institutions because it implies some form of enforcement. The myth of the individual says that each should be his or her own boss and that the individual is not subject to outside influence. Of course the myth is not true and in fact Afrikan Americans are subjected to all kinds of external constraints on behavior, more than their fair share. Examples range from the yoke of slavery through to the modern day abuses of DWB (Driving While Black).

One could reasonably expect Black folk to consciously and unconsciously resist efforts directed at modulating behavior. If collective consciousness precedes institutions, then there will be a certain "surrender" within our people, where they willingly and proactively proceed along the paths established by our institutions. Therefore an agreement is required between Black people and their institutions. This understanding must entail the sharing of trust and the willingness of the people to comply with, and otherwise support, institutional edicts and/or solutions. This might require sacrificing things we hold dear. On the other hand it is not surrender at all since the notion of the primacy of the individual is a lie. Thus, the cost to the individual, in terms of a willingness and a commitment to support institutions through compliance, is minimal. Yet, the benefits to the individual and to the group may be great indeed.

Institutions also should be involved in mediating the intricacies of division of labor, as this concept is applied to a collective. This notion is central since Afrikan Americans are a numerical minority within America. Division of labor is related to efficiency in getting things accomplished. If properly applied, division of labor suggests that Afrikan American institutions can be more agile in support of our culture. Division of labor is also a consideration in extending our areas of interests and spheres of influence to include people of Africa and the African Diaspora. As a community, we must know how many computer programmers, engineers, accountants, teachers, etc., we possess.

3. Coordination, Cooperation, and Communication. Due to the maafa's impact on the interpersonal relationships of Black people, our community is in need of systematic and active approaches that will facilitate coordination, cooperation, and communication. This function should be relegated to all Afrikan American institutions. Specifically, we should design our institutions with the expressed purpose of restoring trust between and among individuals. This task will not be complete until trust rings supreme, until trust is a fact of life, until trust is an unconscious and conscious reality. To achieve this we must turn to our strengths, which are spirit, energy, faith, and forgiveness. Throughout the maafa we have demonstrated these characteristics. We must also turn away from the false gods of ego (i.e., personality apart from soul/spirit) and materialism. Coordination, cooperation, and communication go hand in hand with trust. Together, these attributes are prerequisites to economic participation and wealth creation.

4. *Social Discipline and Diligence.* Discipline and diligence are attributes usually associated with the individual; yet, cultures must be disciplined and diligent as well. The lack of these attributes will surely result in information asymmetry, a lack of cultural follow through upon which trust is built, and cultural chaos. Since institutions are the mechanisms of collective human actions, they represent a method for achieving discipline and diligence within the group. So how do institutions imbue a culture with discipline and diligence? By keeping the collective's "eyes on the prize," by keeping the focus forever on our essential information and objectives. If institutions are disciplined and diligent in their functions (as outlined here), we can reasonably expect that these attributes will translate to the constituents of those institutions. Conventional wisdom suggests that disciplined societies flow from disciplined individuals, however, the process is more circular, more interactive than that. The disciplined individual is a product of his or her (institutional) environment. Be it family, church, or school, institutions play a critical role in establishing a life of discipline and diligence for the individuals and the community.

5. *Teaching and Learning.* Teaching and learning are essential functions in the maintenance of culture. While this role is typically exercised by educational institutions (i.e., schools at all level), it is required of all institutions. Groups of people survive, evolve, and prosper based on their ability to adapt to the environment of which they are a part. In this adaptive process, change is initiated and sustained through the effective use of information. With respect to people, information is passed from generation to generation through the gene and the meme. This is a primary function for institutions.

6. *Preserve Wisdom.* Institutions govern how the collective remembers and forgets. The survival of Afrikan American culture is dependent on the proactive establishment of a knowledge system that embodies our important and essential information. Much of the debate regarding intelligence has to do with the orality-literacy shift and the subordination of culture to technology (the written word and print are technologies). Under the best of circumstances a shift from a primarily oral society to one based on the written word would be daunting, taking perhaps many generations to achieve. America's slaves and their posterity were required to undergo this transition under extreme duress, with the dominant culture deliberately blocking the transition by custom and law.

The transition from orality to literacy is still ongoing for Afrikan Americans. We should not forego orality; rather, our institutions must remind us that American culture is based on the written word, and that fact has important implications and repercussions for us. Irrespective of the form of discourse, our essential information must be captured, placed into context, and maintained.

This is the work of institutions and implies more than a custodial function; it is related ultimately to the preservation of wisdom and is a macro-cultural responsibility. Paradoxically, institutions accomplish this not only by assimilating and managing new and existing information, but also by *excluding* information that is not relevant to the interests and objectives of the culture they serve. By excluding information, institutions protect us from information glut, thus helping us to maintain coherence, meaning, and value in the face of chaos.

7. *Watchdog.* Who is responsible for policing institutions? Who will monitor and negotiate with dominant cultural institutions? American institutions have an abysmal historical record regarding the needs of Afrikan Americans. The degree of this failure can be measured by the degree of disparity that exists in American society. As we build communities, we must build an infrastructure to keep the dominant culture, if not honest, at least aware of its shortcomings. One of the chief responsibilities of elected public officials, particularly state and federal legislative bodies, should be to ensure that the principal community is responsive to the needs of *all* of their constituents. Black public officials should be very focused on the disparity in American life and the commitment of publicly funded institutions to achieving parity. This policing function of the legislature is paramount. Also, we must police our own institutions as they endeavor to pick up the slack when the principal community falls short.

8. *Catalyst for Innovation.* Innovation, in the pursuit of cultural development, offers an opportunity for extraordinary progress in the elimination of disparity within American

society. The enormous benefits of innovation should not
be restricted to the technological or business realms. If
there is a need for cultural development within the Afrikan
American community, then it must come about through
the innovative application of knowledge. Institutions, as
mechanisms for collective human action, should serve as
catalysts for this purpose. We require innovation in each
area of human activity, especially wealth creation. Parity
gives our innovations direction. The degree and variety of
innovation is unlimited because our creativity is unlimited.

Building Blocks for Afrikan American Communities

First and foremost, an Afrikan American community
is a manifestation of our collective African consciousness
as it has evolved in America. If the infrastructure is lacking, it is but a symptom that we have forgotten our collective consciousness. It is the collective consciousness which
informs us regarding the "rules for living." Individuals
can choose to recognize and accept our collective existence as readily as we recognize and accept our individual-
ized existence. If individual Afrikan Americans were to
do this, the result would be the development of community sufficient and necessary to ensure that we survive and
prosper. This would be the path of Spirit. Our task would
be easy, our burdens light. But we are in somewhat of a
quandary, caught within the promise, the seduction, and
the betrayal of the dominant culture's institutions on the
one hand, while worshiping the false idol of individualism on the other hand. We have forgotten our African
legacy. We have forgotten our ancestors and what they
accomplished and endured. We have forgotten that we
are our brother's keeper.

We must therefore undertake the task of remembrance. This task can be achieved as we put in place humanly devised constraints and guidance for living—institutions. For Afrikan American institutions, "the bar is set high." This is so because institutions represent a higher order of human interaction than we have demonstrated to date. It is an evolutionary step that our culture must take now. The eight functions of Afrikan American institutions listed above are hard requirements; they are not negotiable. Our institutions, either singularly or in combination, must exercise *all* of these functions and exercise them well. In the chart below, these considerations are presented as building blocks.

Building Blocks For An Afrikan American Community

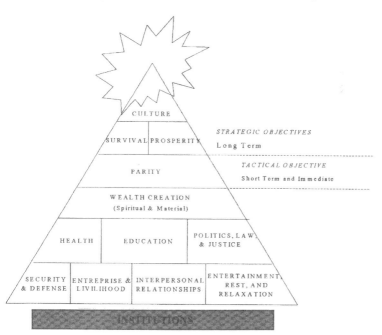

The final consideration in building community is
oneness. Everything is interrelated and connected. The
eight areas of human activity are interdependent and mu-
tually supportive. So are the functions exercised by institutions. But more importantly, the notion of community
implies that our institutions are interdependent and mutu-
ally supportive as well. They should meld together as a
functioning unit. There is a common goal, with common
objectives, all revolving around a common and evolving
knowledge system. Without this, Afrikan American institutions will be ineffective and we, as a people, will fail
to achieve community.

EPILOGUE

We have attempted to provide a framework sufficiently broad in scope to capture and define the complexi-
ties of Afrikan American culture. As we assess our conditions and circumstance, we should use a framework based
on culture, rather than one based on race. This is so because the concept of race is beneficial only to the racist.
For Afrikan Americans, a racist analysis (i.e., one based
on race) is a path to nowhere, to nothingness. The analysis that we have undertaken is a cultural one having to do
with individual as well as collective behavior.

Our analysis is not without historical precedent. As
we consider things past and present, through a cultural
rather than a racist (or racial) motif, we can better appre-
ciate the significance of the many and varied contributions of past generations. Also, we can discern the missed
steps and tactical errors of our forebears. The considerable talents and insights of our ancestors have often been
mired in the fallacy of analysis based on race. Rightly or
wrongly, race occupied a pivotal role in their thoughts and
actions and therefore in our history. Yet, our cultural evolution to this point is but a reflection of our history. The
history of African cultural development in America provides many examples of events to illustrate and reinforce
our updated analytical approach regarding culture, parity,
psychological taxation, and institutions. We will lift out
of time a few examples of Afrikan American experiences
and achievement and place them in the context of this cultural analytical framework.

Those that we highlight are not randomly selected
personalities nor events. Each represents critical periods
in the cultural evolution of African and Afrikan American

culture as well as magnificent contributions by individuals to the cultural collective. Though not chronologically listed, the people and achievements that are highlighted span the time period from Colonial America (Pre American Revolutionary War) through to the Civil Rights Era (1965 with the death of Malcolm X). A critical examination of this long period illustrates that Afrikan American cultural development until the death of Malcolm X was reasonable and steady. This is remarkable considering the fact that the maafa was working steadfastly against our cultural development. The 1954 Brown vs. Board of Education decision sowed the seeds of integration and a misplaced reliance on the institutions of others. The death of Malcolm X signaled the beginning of an extraordinary retrograde in our cultural development; this is when *things* began to *fall apart*. The retrograde in our cultural evolution accelerated out of control with the death of Martin Luther King.

Institutional Resurrection
Examples in Time

> Our cultural evolution in the United States is exemplified in the life and times of the following:
> Culture: **William Henry Sheppard, 1865 - 1927**
> Parity: **Reverend Richard Allen, 1760 - 1831**
> Psychological Taxation: **El-Hajj Malik El-Shabazz, 1925 - 1965**
> Institutional Infrastructure: **Dean Kelly Miller, 1863 - 1939**

Long after their physical death, these ancestors continue to instruct and enlighten us. The events of their lives highlight the significance of culture, the virtues of parity and collective human actions, as well as the critical role of institutions. Each in his own way saw the need to resurrect community.

William Henry Sheppard
The Culture of Colonial Africa, Through Ebony Eyes!

How do we characterize Afrikan American culture? What attributes do we ascribe to it? These are not simple questions, for in America, the land of hatred and self-hatred of Black (i.e., racism as manifested in White and Black), any conception of the cultural Self of Afrikan Americans must be viewed with suspicion and skepticism. As an example, if we allow self-hatred (Black racism) to color our thinking, then we will view our African nature as negative. This would be an error in thinking, for our African essence is our strength and our salvation. As we conceptualize our culture, we must view it from both the individual and the collective perspectives. What is our view of the collective Self? What is the view of our culture at the collective level, and what is the basis of that view? Has our view of our culture been shaped or distorted by external forces (i.e., the dominant culture)? If so, then we need to rebuild our conception of the cultural collective, and we need to start that process at a point in time prior to White interference in African culture.

An examination of the nature of African culture *prior to White interference* reveals a written record that is sparse and inadequate; there exist quantitative and qualitative shortcomings of the record as written, *by Africans*. The written accounts of precolonial African culture are often filtered through the prejudices and biases of White culture and are therefore of little utility to our objectives of cultural understanding and reparation. This is the conventional wisdom regarding depictions of African culture prior to White interference.

Fortunately, other kinds of "records" do exist. They are codified in the collective memory and manifested in orality, rituals, and ceremony as well as sculpture, dance, and other artistic forms. The written record is not the sole, nor the most reliable, means of conveying, or even describing, a culture. The people now called Afrikan Americans are derived from primarily oral cultures of Africa, that is, cultures based on the spoken word rather than the written word. Therefore, a sparse written record can be anticipated.

In *Presbyterian Pioneers in Congo*, Black Presbyterian missionary William Henry Sheppard turns the conventional wisdom on its ear with very detailed, eyewitness written accounts of Black culture in the region of Africa known as the Congo, during the period from 1890 to 1910. In many ways, the story of African and Afrikan American culture is one of interference. It is a story of White interference of nonwhite cultures, a story of cultural development thwarted and distorted from their original form and course, often in grotesque ways. William H. Sheppard provides us a unique and different view of African culture. In *King Leopold's Ghost*, author Adam Hochshild states:

> William Sheppard was the first black American missionary in the Congo. As we listen to him in the book, letters, and magazine articles he writes over the next two decades, and in speeches given to rapt audiences at Hampton and elsewhere while he is on leave, we hear someone strikingly different from almost all the Americans and Europeans who have been to Africa before him. . .

Sheppard was in a place and time to give perhaps a final glimpse of Africa during the rise of the apocalyptic King Leopold of Belgium. The accounts of Sheppard and those of other Afrikan American observers during the same time period stand in bright contrast to most other depictions of African culture. Sheppard lived and worked in Africa as the last vestiges of pristine African culture succumbed to White European colonialism. In Sheppard, the final view of African culture prior to White interference is, ironically, an Afrikan American view. What of the *character* of these cultures? What were they like? Sheppard tells us of his encounters with honest, hard working, and orderly societies. He describes people void of poverty, drunkardness, and contention. He speaks of the customs, traditions, and rituals of the various people with whom he associated as well as remarkable systems of governance. In so doing, he gave us insight into the necessary and sufficient institutions which governed the individual and collective lives of African people. He saw vast lands under cultivation and witnessed elaborate systems of trade and bartering. He saw cultural cohesion and people working toward survival and prosperity.

While the contributions of Black Africa to world civilization is contested only by a few White people, most other people of the world would concede that Africa not only contributed but is the source of civilization. There is an awareness by Afrikan Americans of Africa's glorious past. Even under the onslaught of racism/white supremacy, Black America has *always* maintained an awareness of the contribution of African cultures. In the years since Sheppard's experiences in the Congo regions of Africa, brilliant historians, Black and White, have amassed an impressive body of knowledge regarding the true nature of

African culture. Their efforts serve to make the contributions and achievements of ancient Africa less remote and enable Afrikan Americans to make meaningful cultural connections to our past.

The magnificence that Sheppard witnessed soon faded into the hellish nightmare of colonialism. For the Congo, this nightmare took the form of King Leopold II of Belgium. African culture would be disrupted and distorted in unprecedented ways. Europeans on both sides of the Atlantic began an orgy of death, disease, and destruction directed at the continent of Africa. This orgy is often referred to as the "scramble for Africa." It was formalized in the Berlin Conference of 1884 - 1885 in which Africa was partitioned in accordance with European/American desires and dictates. There was no Black representation at this conference. Greed has fueled pernicious interference in the affairs of Africa, and racism/white supremacy has been the justification or rationale for the greed. The death, destruction and disease left in the wake of the "conquests" of European cultures has eternally altered the very makeup of innumerable nonwhite cultures. The pillage and outright thievery of land, natural resources, and the sovereignty of the cultural "other" have been the hallmark of European "conquests" worldwide These characteristics of White culture are personified in the life and misdeeds of King Leopold. The scope of Leopold's atrocities are hard to imagine. They were on the level of genocide, cutting the population of the Congo region perhaps in half, from 20 million to 10 million. The brutal activities of Leopold sowed the seed to the modern day chaos in the Congo. His sad legacy still remains in the form of the Belgium connections to atrocities in and around Rwanda in the present era.

The life and times of William Sheppard were extraordinary. He contributed to the first worldwide human rights effort aimed at dismantling the personal empire that Leopold had amassed. This personal empire was gained at the expense of Africa and African people. Sheppard also made a direct contribution to Afrikan American culture by allowing us to peer into the inner workings of a segment of African society, prior to large scale interference by external forces. He provides a creditable basis upon which to build a conception of our cultural nature, if that conception is lacking. Due to the insidious and pervasive nature of racism/white supremacy, it is almost a certainty that the Self concept of Afrikan Americans will be lacking. Sheppard described societies where the interests of the individual were subordinated to the interests of the collective; individualism was not an issue.

Our challenge is to build a positive concept of Self in contrast to the false image that racism has perpetuated. Our ancestors have ensured that the knowledge of our Self would remain intact and accessible to us. It requires only our recognition and acceptance. Sheppard and countless other ancestors have preserved the truth even as racism and greed have conspired to bury it. At the collective level, our culture is imbued with the attributes of our Creator. Culture at the collective level is essentially Spirit. Man can not touch nor tarnish this Spirit, but we can be distracted and lose remembrance. Our culture at the collective level is omnipotent, omnipresent, omniscient; it is Love, Peace, Forgiveness. These are the qualities that William Sheppard saw in the people of the Congo region of Africa. W.E.B Dubois saw these same qualities in Afrikan Americans. In *The Gift of Black Folk: The Negroes in the Making of America,* Dubois delineates the "gifts of the Negro" to American society; he sums up our essential character in the following observations regarding the Afrikan American quality called Spirit:

> Above and beyond all that we have mentioned, perhaps least tangible but just as true is the peculiar spiritual quality which the Negro has injected into American life and civilization. It is hard to define or characterize it - a certain spiritual joyousness; a sensuous, tropical love of life, . . .

Richard Allen
A Most Enduring Demonstration of Parity

The African Methodist Episcopal (AME) Church stands prominently in the annals of Afrikan American history. For many, the establishment and maintenance of the AME Church is nothing less than divinely inspired. Its founder, Richard Allen, was part of a remarkable continuum of organizing efforts by free Black men in America after the Revolutionary War. This continuum involved the establishment of the first Black Masonic lodge (African Lodge No. 459, Boston, 1787), the Free African Society (at Philadelphia in 1787), and Black Methodist churches (1791; 1794, Philadelphia). The well known story of the founding of the AME Church is recounted in *Blacks in Colonial America* by Oscar Reiss:

> The African Methodist Episcopal Church (Bethel), founded by Richard Allen, was established following an insult to black worshipers at the Saint George Methodist Episcopal Church in Philadelphia. While on their knees, the blacks were lifted bodily from the "white" area. They left the church, and in 1786 they started a black church that was completed in 1799.

The formation of the AME church was a response to discrimination and disparate treatment of Black people by White people. Noteworthy is that the response was institutional in nature. Churches tend to be institutions unto themselves; that is, they often meet the requirements of being an institution as set forth in the previous chapter. The effectiveness of churches as institution is limited by the number of adherents or members. Indeed within the Afrikan American community, the church stands out as the lone institution easily recognized. The church, or religion, in the Afrikan American community tends to be fractious, with many denominations and varying doctrines. This aspect of the church limits its ability to serve as the basis for collective reform for Afrikan Americans. In this sense, the Church might be a functional institution, but it is only one. Our dilemma is that we require many institutions concerned with all aspects of human activities. It is unlikely that religion in the Black community can ever serve as *the* unifying agent of our people, say in a manner that Judaism serves the Jewish community.

Yet, the Black Church has been the basis from which our most important social and economic initiatives and movements have emerged. In part, this is because the Church was the only place for Black people to meet. The ability of individuals to associate is the strength of this nation. From the basic ability of individuals to meet and to associate flows organizations and thereby, institutions. Black people, slave and free, were not allowed to associate freely. They were, in fact, prohibited from association in most instances. So the church, as a meeting place, assumed an importance rivaled only by, perhaps, food and shelter. The prohibition on free, unencumbered association has served to thwart the overall development of institutions within our community. This legacy also accounts for the fact that churches tend to be the stronger institutions in the Black community.

Nonetheless, the formation of the AME Church is a glorious and prototypical example of an appropriate response to disparity in American society. It is an example in history of what should happen when the institutions of the dominant culture are not responsive to the needs of Black citizens; we should form our own institutions to take up the slack. On a wholesale level, Afrikan Americans today are faced with the same situation which confronted the worshipers at Philadelphia's Saint George Methodist Episcopal Church in 1786. But today, Afrikan Americans receive disparate treatment from the totality of America's institutions, not just the church. The disparity in American society between Afrikan American culture and the dominant culture is the measure of this maltreatment.

As a free man in the North, Richard Allen demonstrated that parity could be achieved through an institutional response to disparity. This was a most repressive era, even for a free or freed Black man. With a view of, and toward, the African collective, Richard Allen brought to bear his considerable skills as a minister and organizer to effect a positive change for African people in America. The AME Church today, with its global reach and impact, stands in testimony to the virtues of culture, parity, and institutions.

El-Hajj Malik El-Shabazz (Malcolm X)
How to Say No to Psychological Taxation

The notion of psychological taxation originated with El-Hajj Malik El-Shabazz (Malcolm X). In word and deed

Malcolm X is perhaps the most vocal and strident opponent to the psychological ill effects of living in America.
More than any other Afrikan American, Malcolm X spoke
to the masses of Black folk and urged us not to buy into
the hype and rhetoric of America's dominant culture. He
taught us to look at the dominant culture critically; he told
us to reject the actions and activities of that culture because it doesn't serve our interests. He extolled us to free
our minds and in so doing lay aside much of the stress and
distress that America would induce in us. In *Martin and
Malcolm and America: A Dream or Nightmare,* author
James H. Cone makes the following observations regarding Malcolm X:

> The first area to consider is black culture and con-
> sciousness. Though both men participated in this
> realm, Malcolm was the towering figure. He was a
> cultural revolutionary who almost singlehandedly
> transformed what black people thought about them-
> selves. He was the progenitor of the black conscious-
> ness movement that emerged during the 1960s, affect-
> ing the whole of black life, including art (black aesthet-
> ics), education (black studies), politics (Black Power)
> and religion (black theology).

Here, Professor Cone does not exaggerate the impact of Malcolm X on Afrikan American culture at the
collective level. His impact at the individual level was
just as dramatic. Professor Cone provides insight into the
nature of this impact:

> Hearing Malcolm analyze the dreadful psychological
> consequences of black self-hate had a transforming
> effect upon the consciousness of African-Americans.
> They began to *think* black and *act* black, because
> Malcolm, through the power of his oratory, helped

them to realize and to accept their *blackness* as the essential element in the definition of their humanity. 'All of us are black first,' he told African-Americans, 'and everything else second.'

To the degree that the terms "black" and "blackness" are cultural designations rather than racial ones, Professor Cone is correct. The terms African (in America) and African-ness could be substituted for black and blackness, respectively (and respectfully). Professor Cone makes this important distinction in the balance of his presentation, omitted here.

In an essay entitled *"The Legacy of Malcolm X,"* author Oba T'Shaka renders the following:

> Malcolm taught us to remove fear from our hearts and follow the example of our ancestors. He constantly taught us about Toussaint, Nat Turner, Denmark Vesey, and Marcus Garvey because he wanted us to model ourselves after them. Malcolm courageously called for self-defense in the early sixties when the civil rights movement was following a policy of turn-the-other-cheek. It took courage for Malcolm to speak the truth no matter what the price. This fearless dedication to the truth was his greatest strength.

Malcolm X made it his primary mission to address miseducation, self-hatred, and their psychological implications for Black America. He confronted the psychological tax head on. It was necessary to rid Afrikan Americans of their psychological burdens, to deliver their minds from bondage, before any other progress could be made. Malcolm X understood the extent of the psychological and miseducation problem of Afrikan Americans. In his autobiography, during the last year of his life, he states:

> I must be honest. Negroes—Afro-Americans—showed
> no inclination to rush to the United Nation and demand
> justice for themselves here in America. I really had
> known in advance that they wouldn't. The American
> white man has so thoroughly brainwashed the black
> man to see himself as only a domestic "civil rights"
> problem that it will probably take longer than I live
> before the Negro sees that the struggle of the American
> black man is international. (*The Autobiography of
> Malcolm X*, Alex Haley)

As he lived, the message of Malcolm was not received
with opened arms by the masses of individual Black people.
Certainly those who heard him were impacted and often
converted. But there was a great deal of fear in the Black
community regarding Malcolm X and his message. It is
ironic that this man of courage induced fear in White and
Black people alike. Ossie Davis eulogized:

> . . .Malcolm, as you can see, was refreshing excite-
> ment; he scared hell out of the rest of us, bred as we
> are to caution, to hypocrisy in the presence of white
> folks, to the smile that never fades. Malcolm knew
> that every white man in America profits directly or
> indirectly from his position vis-a'-vis Negroes, prof-
> its from racism even though he does not practice it
> or believe in it.

Davis implies that Malcolm X induced fear, not because he was frightening but, because we were fearful.
Fear, held by individuals, is a major component of psychological taxation. Malcolm X challenged our fears and
before our eyes, exhibited the courage of his convictions;
he "walked the talk!" Aside from Malcolm X's dramatic
impact on individuals, there was and is a collective aspect

of his words and his work. Malcolm X's words and ideas seem to flow through our community like a contagion. Whether or not one is receptive to these ideas, the ideas seem to persist and sooner or later you are infected. Or perhaps, you are inoculated. Inoculated against self-hatred and fear. Malcolm X recognized that our essential challenge in America was at the collective level. Upon returning to the U.S. from his second trip to Africa, he talked about his evolving attitude toward white people:

> It was in the Holy World that my attitude was changed, by what I experienced there, and by what I witnessed there, in terms of brotherhood—not just brotherhood toward me but brotherhood between all men of all nationalities and complexions, who were there and now that I am back in America, my attitude here concerning white people has to be governed by what my black brothers and I experience here, and what we witness here—in terms of brotherhood.

Continuing, Malcolm X cuts to the essence of the problem then, and more so, now:

> The problem here in America is that we meet such asmall minority of individual so-called 'good,' or 'brotherly' white people. Here in the United States, notwithstanding those few 'good' white people, it is the *collective* 150 million white people whom the *collective* 22 million black people have to deal with!

> Why, here in America the seeds of racism are so deeply rooted in the white people collectively, their belief that they are 'superior' in some way is so deeply rooted, that these things are in the national subconsciousness. Many whites are even unaware of their own racism, until they face some test, and then their racism emerges in one form or another.

Here, Malcolm X acknowledges that our true challenge is at the collective level of culture. We would contend that this is our age old challenge, from the start of slavery to the present day.

Our enduring leaders are the ones who speak to the collective urge within our culture. It is the enduring or eternal quality of people, places, and events which alert us to our divinity. Malcolm X is one of those timeless leaders. His words uttered three decades ago still ring true today. This is so because we have not taken up the challenge that he put before us. With his rhetoric, Malcolm X prodded and admonished us to view the dominant culture's tactics of oppression and domination as that—tactics. He knew that with awareness, tactics can be countered and made null. In the years since his murder, white domination and oppression have undergone a metamorphosis. It has become more insidious, more virulent, more systemic, and more structured. The disparity between Afrikan American culture and America's dominant culture attests to these facts. At the same time, we have become almost obsessed with individualism and less capable of extending our collective consciousness into the world. Collective consciousness and self-awareness are the prizes that Malcolm X gave us. But we have not put in place the mechanisms to propagate this consciousness or awareness to all members of our culture. To this end we do an injustice and a disservice to ourselves and to the memory and efforts of Malcolm X and all other ancestors. It is ironic that Malcolm X, who eased our psychological tax burden in such a profound and lasting way, would himself be caught in the vortex of psychological taxation on a personal level with the threat of physical death heaped upon him and his family. While he was undoubtedly prepared for the twist of fate, the price he paid must not be in vain.

Dean Kelly Miller
The Negro Sanhedrin—Seeds of Community

The Negro Sanhedrin was an organizing effort which took place in 1924. It was arguably as close as Afrikan Americans have come to developing a community in America. This Race Conference sought to bring Afrikan American social, economic, and civil rights organizations under a single coordinating body established by those organizations. Dean Kelly Miller of Howard University spearheaded this comprehensive approach to cultural development. Clearly, the founders of this significant movement saw the need for Afrikan Americans to organize at a level higher than "individual" organizations They recognized the need for some form of division of labor in order to address the "race problem." Most importantly, they recognized and accepted the notion that Africans in America exist as a collective and must act accordingly. In its intent and scope, the Negro Sanhedrin set the historical precedent for the resurrection of an Afrikan American community.

In *The Negro Sanhedrin, A Call to Conference*, issued in early 1923, Kelly Miller explains the term Sanhedrin in some detail:

> The Sanhedrin was the Jewish assembly. The Great Sanhedrin was composed of seventy-one members with supreme jurisdiction. The Lesser Sanhedrin, composed of twenty-three members, represented each province with local and limited jurisdiction. Similarity of situation suggest a like conference of the Negro people of the United States to-day under the ancient designation. The Greater Sanhedrin with nation-wide function, and the Lesser Sanhedrin limited to city and local jurisdiction, also suggest a happy comparison.

It is both prophetic and ironic that Miller selected the Sanhedrin model as an organizing vehicle, since the present work would contend that globally, Jewish culture is prototypical of how a cultural collective should operate. Obviously, this fact was not lost to the organizers of the Negro Sanhedrin. The notion of a Greater and Lesser Sanhedrin is roughly analogous to the collective and individual aspects of culture as outlined in the present work. The Negro Sanhedrin offers additional background information:

> The All-Race Conference, commonly known as the Negro Sanhedrin, has been called to convene in the city of Chicago, during the week of February 11, 1924. The civil rights bodies which joined in the issuance of the call are: The National Association for the Advancement of Colored People, The Equal Rights League, The Race Congress, The Blood Brotherhood, The Inter-national Uplift League and the Friends of Negro Freedom.

The shear number of organizations represented at the Sanhedrin was testimony to the stature of Kelly Miller, Alain Locke, and the other organizers. The 15 February 1924 edition of the Afro American newspaper carried the headlines: "500 DELEGATES AT SANHEDRIN IN CHICAGO" and "Nearly Every Big Organization Represented at Five-Day All Race Congress." The accompanying article stated in part:

> There are seventy-five or more national organizations of the colored race," said Prof. Miller. "If we can get a unit plan of action, the general result will be the betterment of the race. The Sanhedrin is not now concerned with action on any specific matter but to get at a common basis of action so that all agencies

will be strengthened in their particular field. This movement is the first of the kind ever undertaken by the race in this country. . . .

The organizers of the Sanhedrin were concerned with establishing a mechanism or framework for collective action. While this goal was laudable, the concept of race does not offer any basis for such a framework. This fact would not have been obvious a mere 60 years after the end of slavery. Likewise, for the Sanhedrin not to be "concerned with action on any specific matter . . ." while *tactically* sound would appear to have been a *strategic* error. Perhaps intergroup politics dictated this approach. Even with the success of the Negro Sanhedrin in his ledger, Kelly Miller in his regular Afro American column of May 16, 1924, states:

> The American Negro is floundering about as a fish out of water or as a sheep without a shepherd. There is not now, nor can there be any effective race leadership until the race determines where it wishes to be led. There must be formulated an aim and ideal toward which the whole group is impelled to move. Miller continues:

> No such ideal has yet been formulated, with the possible exception of the African repatriation which is so ardently advocated by Marcus Garvey. This idea was not originated by Mr. Garvey, but merely adopted and adapted by him. It is as old as the colonization scheme.

> The only new feature added is that the movement should be directed by the Negro himself, and not by the manipulation of white philanthropists as all previous proposals have been. Here is indeed set up a definite and well understood objective. The chief

objective is that it is not practical and does not commend itself to the sensibilities of the vast majority of the Afro-American people.

The above commentary is very telling. First, he comments on the major factor limiting the scope of the Garvey movement. The movement had as its objective the wholesale return of Black people to Africa. Miller correctly assesses that "the vast majority" of Black people did not abide in this objective. Coming only three months after the monumental Negro Sanhedrin, Kelly Miller seems resigned to the fact that the implementation of the ideals achieved at the All-Race Conference would be problematic. Aspects of the problem included the reluctance of constituent organizations to submit to the edicts of an overarching council, the administrative and procedural complications arising from an attempt to coordinate the activities of organizations nationwide, and most importantly, the lack of a unifying theme capable of resonating with the masses of Black folk.

The Negro Sanhedrin was not without benefit or positive outcome. The effort represented unanimity among Afrikan American leaders that a higher order of organization was required if the Afrikan American collective was to survive and prosper. Recommendations, adopted and implemented, were contained in the Commission Report:

(1) The Sanhedrin would continue on a permanent basis,
(2) An Executive Council of the Sanhedrin would be maintained in Washington, D.C., and
(3) The Sanhedrin project "in no way compromises the individual independence or infringes upon the special activities of constituent organizations, ..."

Other recommendations flowed from the several committees of the Conference. Those committees included Health, Education, the Press, Race Movements (Domestic and Foreign), Fraternal Organizations, Religion, Inter-Racial Relations, Politics and Public Utterance, Woman's Movements and Organization, Labor, Business, Race Knowledge and Promotion of Scholarship, Music, Literature and Art, and the College Youth. A treatment of the Negro Sanhedrin is found in Harold Cruse's *Plural But Equal: A Critical Study of Blacks and Minorities and America's Plural Society.*

Dean Kelly Miller was an extraordinary talent and intellectual. He was a strong voice, providing straightforward political and social commentary on the conditions and circumstances of the Black community throughout his life. He served as a kind of consciousness for Afrikan America. As with all great Afrikan American leaders, he recognized and accepted the spiritual truth of the existence of an African collective. He sought a mechanism for its manifestation. In the contemporary accounts of the life of Kelly Miller seldom is the Negro Sanhedrin mentioned. Mentioned is his enduring work as a scholar at Howard University or the fact that he was the first Black man to attend John Hopkins University. Yet in terms of contributions to African and Afrikan American culture, the Negro Sanhedrin stands as a monumental achievement.

Perhaps the Negro Sanhedrin took place too early in Afrikan American cultural evolution to gain traction. There were competing efforts and movements (i.e., Marcus Garvey and the Universal Negro Improvement Association, the NAACP, and others) which undoubtedly siphoned off support and attention. In other ways, the political, economic, and technological environments were not optimized

to support such an expansive undertaking.   More likely
however, is the sobering fact that a race-based analysis
and concomitant plans and actions are doomed to failure.
We can accept it as a basic truth; the concept of race is
only beneficial to the racist. While the Negro Sanhedrin
may be an example of community deferred, it represented
an excellent model in all respects. We are sufficiently
along in our cultural development to reconsider and re-
visit the important issues represented in the Sanhedrin ini-
tiative.

An Intergenerational Appeal

AFRIKAN AMERICAN GENERATIONS
SINCE THE 13TH AMENDMENT 1865

Born Between	Generation Since 13th Amed.
1865 - 1895-------------------	1st Generation
1895 - 1925 -----------------	2nd Generation
1925 - 1955 -----------------	**3rd Generation**
1955 - 1985 -----------------	4th Generation
1985 - 2015 -----------------	5th Generation

By some accounts, a generation spans a period of
thirty years. Those within my generation were born between the years 1925 to 1955; we are the *third generation*
after the Thirteenth Amendment to the U.S. Constitution
ended "formal" slavery. The Afrikan American generation represented by this group of men and women would
be between the ages of 45 and 75 years old. While this
generation has witnessed, participated in, and brought
about some tremendous social and economic changes to
the benefit of American and Afrikan American cultures,
it has also failed generations succeeding it.

My generation failed to provide to succeeding Afrikan American generations (i.e., 4th generation and 5th generation) a viable community. This is a contemporary failure. It is in fact still in progress. By contrast, the generations before my generation, say the generations of DuBois and Malcolm X, left my generation in good stead. They provided a functional, if nascent, community of institutions which insured that my generation was educated, that it survived, and that it would prosper. They insured that mechanisms were in place to modulate and mold behavior. These mechanisms include family, church, and a sense of community (through a collective memory). I contend that my generation failed to do these minimal things for the generations that follow us. The factors that led to such a failure are both internal and external to our culture. The purpose of this appeal is to recognize the failure, identify its causes, and to gain a commitment from those in my generation, and those in preceding and succeeding generations, to fix the problem. Hence, it is an intergenerational appeal.

The present day ills of the Afrikan American community are the direct result of a lack of viable institutions. There is a lack in quantity and quality/functionality. In deed Afrikan Americans made steady, often impressive, gains toward the maintenance of institutions until the recent past. These gains are chronicled in our history. It was about the time of the death of Malcolm X that our institutions were relegated to "back burner" status; we began to omit Black institutions from our considerations in favor of a misplaced reliance on the institutions of America's dominant culture. This critical act of omission effectively truncated the possibility of "equality" in America for individual Afrikan Americans, not just for my generation but for succeeding ones also. It guaranteed the persistence of disparity between cultures within this country.

The conscious or subconscious reliance on White institutions by Afrikan Americans is an internal failing which weakens our community; this is an intragroup factor. There were external factors that work to undermine Black institutions as well. The Vietnam War was devastating to the Afrikan American community. The death and casualty rates of this war were borne disproportionately by the disenfranchised of American society. The war negatively affected the primary institution of the Afrikan American community—family. The fathers and would-be fathers of Black families were taken away or taken out, leaving a void never to be filled. A second external factor impacting the formation and maintenance of our institutions is government-sponsored programs. Some of these take the form of policies, laws, and other "helpful" interventions. Other governmental programs were designed to deliberately undermine and de-stabilize the Black community ostensibly "in the interests of national security." Typically, these programs were implemented via military and/or intelligence/investigative agencies of the U.S. government. Most notorious among these programs was (is) the so called COINTELPRO (counterintellegence program) operated out of the Department of Justice by the Federal Bureau of Investigation. These government sponsored programs often work outside and above the law. They entailed gross abuses of the civil and human rights of individual and groups. These abuses have continued, but more importantly, they contributed directly to the current environment of *prosecutorial fascism*. Prosecutorial fascism is a law "enforcement" phenomenon involving an unholy alliance between prosecutors and police, where the systematic and sustained force of "legal" power is directed against individuals and classes of people based on race, politics, and other discriminators. Prosecutorial fascism has led to the increased and disparate incarceration rate of Afrikan Americans, rampant racial profiling throughout the law enforcement community, the murder and abuse of innocent citizens by the police, etc. The ill effects of prosecutorial fascism are not restricted to the Black community; witness the failed American coup d'etat, under guise of a presidential impeachment.

Legislators and courts at both the state and federal levels have systematically undermined the development of a Black community. Their approach and effect, while less covert, is just as insidious and injurious. The implementation of the so-called "welfare" system is the classic example. The much maligned welfare system is an invention of the dominant culture; it was neither designed nor implemented by Black people. Black people were not primary beneficiaries, White people were. Yet the implementation and enforcement of welfare regulations served to destabilize Black families and, thus, the whole community.

Our lack of a community, therefore, is not an accident. The dominant culture is threatened by the notion of Black solidarity, and enlists the power of its institutions to undercut this possibility on a regular and continuing basis. These are aspects of some of the external forces arrayed to thwart our realization of a collective consciousness; yet, these pale in comparison to the internal factors which are our sole responsibility.

The failure to provide viable institutions is the most striking legacy of the Black community's pursuit of integration. Perhaps we thought of integration as a remedy for economic and social injustice in American society. The remedy failed and the nature of the failure is utterly unique in human history in that it occurred within a single generation and it dealt with the institutions of the community which are the substance, the glue, that would bind a community, or not.

No other cultural or ethnic group in America has made such tragic strategic error. The institutional battlefield of Black America is littered with the corpses of dead or defunct businesses, neighborhoods, and relationships. All of this resting on a strategic blunder, the enormity of which is still largely unrecognized. The discussion of the intergenerational failure is not a fault finding mission; rather it is the beginning of an ameliorative process. It is a genuine appeal to address the spiritual challenge that is before us. It is a spiritual challenge because by "definition" culture at the collective level is Spirit! It is also an appeal to come to grips with the reality of American life. That reality is that America is a land of institutions and associations. Institutions govern the collective life of this nation. The generation 45-75 years of age have concerned itself with the ruse of individual pursuits, having very little regard or recognition of the reality of the Afrikan American collective. It is not a fault-finding mission because this generation was ill-prepared to take up the challenge of cultural maintenance and development. With the blind spot of individualism governing our lives, the culture of Afrikan Americans has been left exposed to influence and manipulation by sophisticated and pernicious forces conspiring in a high stakes game of cultural domination.

At the core of this appeal is the belief that the failure can be remedied. However, it requires an admission that a grave mistake was made and an understanding of the nature of the mistake.

Secondly, it requires an intergenerational partnership willing to work toward amelioration. The central objective must be the restoration of viable institutions within our communities. To remedy the intergenerational failure, we must put aside the (institutional) "eaches" and try to come to grips with the (institutional) whole. This is a difficult thing to do. The education system of the dominant culture is the basis of our own education. It is based on de-constructionism, breaking things down and destroying them to "understand" them. Often times, we can't even imagine the whole of our culture outside the context of America's dominant culture. We tend to succumb to European method(s) of analysis, which is an aspect of the individualist mindset. Yet, to remedy our intergenerational failure we must seek a balance between the individual mindset and due consideration of the collective.

Just as Gil Scott Heron admonished, "the revolution will not be televised," the remedy for what ails Black America will not lend itself to sound bites or cursory examination, even though American conventions and mindset seem to demand this. We must elevate our thinking and actions to another level. We must understand that we can be multifaceted and that we can think and act strategically. If we are willing to look at things a little differently, and invest a little of ourselves, we can realize tremendous benefits. What is required is that we willingly exercise the facilities necessary to discern the hidden aspects of our collective life in America. These include the remembrance and acceptance of the collective (i.e., the collective aspect of our culture, our oneness in Spirit); the importance of an African knowledge system; the logic and essential nature of institution building; and the necessity of community as a manifestation of our culture.

So, the intergenerational appeal calls for a pact between Afrikan American generations now inhabiting the world. The pact asserts our undying commitment to providing mechanisms for collective human actions. It should be a binding agreement on our part to recognize and accept that, in culture as in spirit, we are one African people living in America. The implication of this oneness is collective consciousness; we are a distinct culture in America's pluralistic society. As such, we have a distinct knowledge system that is related not only to our conditions and circumstances, but to our collective consciousness as well. We are co-owners, builders, and participants in the "general" knowledge system of American culture; we can certainly do the same for our own African culture. We assert that we have cultural objectives which are survival and prosperity in the long term and parity in the short term. We direct our individual and collective behavior toward the manifestation of these objectives. Never again shall a generation of young people be placed in a situation of not having strong institutions to modulate and mold behavior. Never again shall we be defenseless in the face of racism/white supremacy and greed. Never again shall our people be solely dependent on the nonresponsive institutions of another's culture. These are the minimal things that a generation must do to prepare the way for generations that follow; as we build communities that consist of institutions grounded in Afrikan American culture.

BIBLIOGRAPHY

Afrika, Llaila O. *African Holistic Health*. Maryland:

Adesegun, Johnson and Koram Publishers,1989.

Akbar, Na'im. *Chains and Images of Psychological Slavery*. Jersey City, NJ: New Mind Productions, 1984.

Akbar, Na'im. *The Community of Self (Revised)*. Tallahassee, FL: Mind Production & Assoc., 1985.

Ani, Marimba. *Yurugu: An African-centered Critique of European Cultural Thought and Behavior*. Trenton, NJ: Africa World Press, Inc., 1994.

Armah, Ayi Kwei. *Two Thousands Seasons*. Oxford: Heinemann Educational, 1973.

Asante, Molefi Kete. *The Afrocentric Idea*. Philadelphia: Temple University Press, 1987.

Bonner, John T. *The Evolution of Culture in Animals*. Princeton. NJ: Princeton University Press, 1980.

Berlin, Ira and Hoffman, Ronald. *Slavery and Freedom in the Age of the American Revolution*. Charlottesville: University Press of Virginia, 1983.

Cone, James H. *Martin & Malcolm & America: A Dream or A Nightmare*. Maryknoll, New York: Orbis Books, 1991.

Cross, Theodore. *The Black Power Imperative: Racial Inequality and the Politics of Nonviolence*. New York: Faulkner Books, 1987.

Cruse, Harold. *The Crisis of the Negro Intellectual: A Historical Analysis of the Failure of Black Leadership.* New York: Quill, 1967.

Cruse, Harold. *Plural but Equal.* New York: William Morrow and Company, Inc., 1987.

Davidson, Basil. *The African Genius: An Introduction to African Cultural and Social History.* Boston, MA: Little, Brown and Company, 1969.

DeCaro, Louis A. *On the Side of My People: A Religious Life of Malcolm X.* New York: New York University Press, 1996.

Delany, Martin R. *The Origin of Races and Color.* Philadelphia, PA: Harper & Brother, Publishers, 1879.

Diop, Cheikh Anta. *Civilization or Barbarism: An Authentic Anthropology.* Brooklyn, NY: Lawrence Hill Books, 1981.

Dolan, Edwin G. and Lindsey, David E. *Economics.* Fort Worth: The Dryden Press, 1994.

Douglas, Mary. *How Institutions Think.* Syracuse, NY: Syracuse University Press, 1986.

Durham, William H. *Coevolution: Genes, Culture, and Human Diversity.* Stanford: Stanford University Press, 1991.

Finch III, Charles S. *Echoes of the Old Darkland: Themes from the African Eden.* Decatur, GA.: Khenti, Inc., 1993.

Freire, Paulo. *Pedagogy of the Oppressed.* New York: The Continuum Publishing Company, 1990.

Fukuyama, Francis. *Trust: The Social Virtues and the Creation of Prosperity*. New York: The Free Press, 1995.

Fuller, Jr., Neely. *The United Independent Compensatory Code/System/Concept: A Textbook/Workbook for Thought, Speech and/or Action for Victims of Racism (White Supremacy)*. Self Published, 1969.

Greenberg, Jack. *Race Relations and American Law*. New York: Columbia University Press, 1959.

Gwaltney, John Langston. *Drylongso: A Self-Portrait of Black America*. New York: Vantage Books, 1981.
Hacker, Andrew. *Two Nations: Black and White, Separate, Hostile, Unequal*. New York: Ballantine Books, 1992.

Hakim, Ida and Fardan, Dorothy Blake and Moritz, Len and Hakeem, Jamil. *Reparations, the Cure for America's Race Problem*. Hampton, VA: U.B. & U.S. Communication Systems, 1994.

Haley, Alex and Malcolm X. *The Autobiography of Malcolm X*. New York: Ballantine Books, 1965.

Hall, Edward T. *Beyond Culture*. New York: Doubleday & Company, Inc., 1976.

Hare, Nathan. *The Black Anglo-Saxons*. Chicago: Third Wold Press, 1991

Harris, Joseph E. *Global Dimensions of The African Diaspora*. Washington, DC: Howard University Press, 1982.

Hayek, Friedrich A. *Individualism and Economic Order*. Chicago: The University of Chicago Press, 1948.

Hazlitt, Henry. *Economics In One Lesson*. New York: Crown Trade Paperbacks, 1962.

Henry, Charles P. *Culture and African American Politics*. Indianapolis: Indiana University Press, 1990.

Hochschild, Adam. *King Leopold's Ghost: A Story of Greed, Terror, and Heroism in Colonial Africa*. Boston: Houghton Mifflin Company, 1999.

Horne, Gerald. *Reversing Discrimination: The Case for Affirmative Action.* New York: International Publishers, 1992.

Hughes, Langston and Bontemps, Arna. *The Book of Negro Folklore*. New York: Dodd, Mead & Company, 1958.

Israel, Arturo. *Institutional Development: Incentives to Performance*. Baltimore: The Johns Hopkins University Press, 1987.

James, George G. M. *Stolen Legacy: The Greeks Were not the Authors of Greek Philosophy, but the People of North Africa, Commonly Called the Egyptians*. San Francisco: Julian Richardson Associates, 1954.

Jochannan ben-, Yosef. *Cultural Genocide in the Black & African Studies Curriculum.* New York: ECA Associates, 1989.
King, Richard. *African Origin of Biological Psychiatry*. Germantown, TN: Seymour-Smith, Inc., 1990.

Kly, Y.N. *International Law and the Black Minority in the U.S.* Atlanta: Clarity Press, Inc., 1990.

Kunjufu, Jawanza. *Black Economics: Solutions for Economic and Community Empowerment*. Chicago: African American Images, 1991.

Latif, Sultan A. and Latif, Naimah. *Slavery: The African American Psychic Trauma*. Chicago: Latif Communications Group, Inc., 1994.

Linnemann, Russell J. *Alain Locke: Reflections on a Modern Renaissance Man*. Baton Rouge: Louisiana State University, 1982.

Lumumba, Chokwe. *Reparations Yes!: The Legal and Political Reasons Why New Afrikans - Black People In North America - Should Be Paid Now For The Enslavement of Our Ancestor*. Washington DC: The House of Songhay Commission for Positive Education, 1987.

Martin, Tony. *The Pan-African Connection: From Slavery to Garvey and Beyond*. Dover, MA: The Majority Press, 1983. Miller, Kelly. *The Negro Sanhedrin: A Call to Conference*. Pamphlet: 1923.

Mises von, Ludwig. *Human Action: A Treatise on Economics*. New York: The Foundation for Economic Education, Inc., 1949.

North, Douglass C. *Institutions, Institutional Change and Economic Performance*. Cambridge, MA: Cambridge University Press, 1990.

Ong, Walter J. *Orality & Literacy: The Technologizing of the Word*. London: Routledge, 1983.

Postman, Neil. *Technopoly: The Surrender of Culture to Technology*. New York: Vintage Books, 1992.

Rand, Ayn. *Capitalism: The Unknown Ideal*. New York: The Penguin Group, 1946.

Redding, Saunders. *They Came in Chains: Americans from Africa.* New York: J.B. Lippincott Company, 1950.

Reiss, Oscar. *Blacks in Colonial America.* Jefferson, NC: McFarland & Company, Inc., 1997.

Rojas, Don. *One People, One Destiny: The Caribbean and Central America Today.* New York: Pathfinder, 1988.

Shapiro, Harry L. *Aspects of Culture.* New Brunswick, NJ: Rutgers University Press, 1957.

Soddy, Frederick. *Wealth, Virtual Wealth and Debt: The Solution of the Economic Paradox.* London: George Allen & Unwin Ltd., 1926.

Stuckey, Sterling. *Slave Culture: Nationalist Theory & the Foundations of Black America.* Oxford: Oxford University Press, 1987.

Schwaller de Lubicz, R.A. *The Temple in Man: Sacred Architecture and the Perfect Man.* Rochester, VT: Inner Traditions International, 1949.

Schwaller de Lubicz, R.A. *Symbol and the Symbolic: Ancient Egypt, Science, and the Evolution of Consciousness.* Rochester, VT: Inner Traditions International, 1949.

Segal, Ronald. *The Black Diaspora: Five Centuries of the Black Experience Outside Africa.* New York: Farrar, Straus and Giroux, 1995.

Swan, L. Alex. *Survival and Progress: The Afro-American Experience.* Westport: CT. Greenwood Press, 1981.

Van Sertima, Ivan. *Great Black Leader: Ancient and Modern.* New Jersey: Journal of African Civilizations, 1988.

Vega, Marta Moreno and Greene, Cheryll Y. *Voices from the Battlefront: Achieving Cultural Equity*. Trenton, New Jersey: Africa World Press, Inc., 1993.

Welsing, Frances Cress. *The Isis Papers: The Keys to the Colors*. Chicago: Third World Press, 1991.

Wilson, William Julius. *The Truly Disadvantaged: The Inner City, the Underclass, and Public Policy*. Chicago: The University of Chicago Press, 1987.

Windsor, Rudolph R. *The Valley of the Dry Bones: The Conditions That Face Black People in America*. New York: Vantage Press, 1986.

Woodson, Carter Godwin. *The Mis-Education of the Negro*. Chicago: African American Images, 2000.

NOTES

NOTES